In the early days of Covid-19, Chris Joffe's unique insights and guidance helped school leaders plan weeks ahead. In *All Clear*, the tools and strategies he teaches will make it possible for school communities to anticipate and prepare for the unpredictable years in advance.

—Steven Lorch, Head of School, Kadima Day School, Los Angeles

Chris Joffe is the kind of person you call when you have only one call to make—a Sherpa in the wilds of crisis response. *All Clear* blends Joffe's EMT urgency with his CEO vision, a must for modern-day risk management.

—Duncan Lyon, Head of School, Allen-Stevenson School

Chris Joffe's book is a tutorial on how to master panic and turn crisis into calm. The secrets he shares in *All Clear* focus on the real-life lessons he learned about the value of working with the people around you, not in spite of them. From the time he was plucked from his mother's arms and dropped into foster care at the age of five, Chris Joffe clearly has been mastering how to communicate and empower people around him during a crisis. You will want to join him after reading *All Clear*.

—Katherine Schweit, former agent and executive for the FBI
and author of the book Stop the Killing,
How to End the Mass Shooting Crisis

An impressive addition to the field of school safety and crisis management, *All Clear* offers invaluable insight and actionable information. With an incredible backstory, Chris Joffe incorporates his personal history with his professional experience to provide a powerful guide for emergency preparedness and crisis response. Written by a true leader in the field; I highly recommend this book.

—Nancy Zarse, PsyD, forensic psychologist and CEO and
founder of Zarse Psychological Services

All Clear

All Clear

Lessons from a Decade Managing School Crises

Chris Joffe

JB JOSSEY-BASS™
A Wiley Brand

For general information on our other products and services or for technical support, please contact our Customer Care Department within the United States at (800) 762-2974, outside the United States at (317) 572-3993 or fax (317) 572-4002.

Wiley also publishes its books in a variety of electronic formats. Some content that appears in print may not be available in electronic formats. For more information about Wiley products, visit our web site at www.wiley.com.

Library of Congress Cataloging-in-Publication Data is Available:

ISBN 9781394178070 (Cloth)
ISBN 9781394178094 (ePDF)
ISBN 9781394178087 (ePUB)

Cover Design: Wiley

Cover Image: © IP Galanternik D.U./Getty

Images © BRPH/Getty Images

SKY10056759_100323

This book is dedicated to those society failed to protect. I'm profoundly sorry. I will fight to protect you and others until I have no fight left. I'll do so through advocacy, training, financial resources, and every other mechanism created in my lifetime. I hope others will join me in that effort. My mission in life is to create a safer world—one that doesn't leave children vulnerable, fighting for their lives. We can do better. We must do better. We deserve better.

Contents

Preface

F. Scott Fitzgerald once said, "The test of a first-rate intelligence is the ability to hold two opposed ideas in the mind at the same time, and still retain the ability to function. One should, for example, be able to see that things are hopeless and yet be determined to make them otherwise."[1]

After Parkland, schools across the country sought solutions in search of doing something to make themselves safer. In too many cases, schools either went it alone or went quickly to achieve solutions that would placate nervous parents. (Though that sounds critical, I don't mean to be. I get it.) In some cases, a rush to arm security or staff a police officer on campus, in others to place fences around the campus. These things all might be useful under the right circumstances and rolled out thoughtfully. In too many cases, the solution itself became the problem. In some cases, the solutions were lethal. I'll share one of those stories with you, about a seven-year-old named Aaron. A school installed a fence in order to mitigate the risk of someone running onto campus to cause harm. For what I believe to be the best intentions, the school moved quickly and the vendor did too. However, during recess, the fence snapped and killed Aaron. The very tool that was designed to cause safety wound up causing harm. It pains me to say this, but my team and I live these stories day in and day out. So, yes, I want you to take action as you read this book. Get a pen and paper, build a checklist, galvanize your community toward action, but note that this book—everything I do—is about taking measured action, calculated to mitigate unintended consequences.

Here's a second one. On a flight from LAX to Atlanta, I received this text from a client. "Federal Law Enforcement

---

[1] February 1936, *Esquire*, "The Crack-Up: A desolately frank document from one for whom the salt of life has lost its savor by F. Scott Fitzgerald," start p. 41, quote p. 41, column 1, Esquire Inc., Chicago, Illinois (Esquire archive at classic.esquire.com).

[agency redacted] need to arrest one of our parents." Here was another critical moment. The risks related to an on-campus takedown are significant. The implications of saying no to federal law enforcement are, too. This book is about building relationships enabling you to do what we did: partner with them so as to handle the arrest elsewhere.

Finally, I often look inward when starting to solve a problem, so here's one I hope you'll enjoy. Thanksgiving Day, quite some time ago, I was at my parents' house along with a handful of other guests. My mom shrieks (never a good sign), and I look over to see the oven on fire. Apparently, the marshmallows on the top of the sweet potato dish had cooked a bit too long. I went over, grabbed the fire extinguisher, and walked toward the oven. She yelled, "Don't you dare!" I was confused and responded, "Put out the fire?" *What's the alternative? Watch the house burn down?* I thought to myself. . .

So who's in charge? Me, who has the training and experience to know that left unaddressed, this oven fire is capable of burning the whole house down, or Mom, because, well, she's Mom? This book is about reaching a conclusion to that question. In our schools, as you'll find later on in your reading, there's a tension between the traditional or "normal" leader of the school and those who either are the crisis leaders or think they should be. We had a more dramatic version of this story play out when two administrators struggled to decide which one was in charge in the midst of an active shooter that was near, but not at, the school in question. The two administrators jockeyed for authority for about 15 minutes while no decisive action was taken. It's as if they were in the kitchen, fire extinguisher in hand, fire burning, and they fought about the next step rather than taking it. Worse, it's more common than you might realize, but we'll find the solutions to that problem together through this book. And, if you were wondering, Mom remained in charge on Thanksgiving. I eventually managed to put the fire out with a watering can, and we had what turned out to be excellent—albeit smoky—sweet potatoes for dinner.

This book will detail stories like Aaron's, which I hope we can eliminate in time, and stories like that text message, which I hope can become the norm for schools and communities across the United States and around the world.

On gun violence. As of the date of the publishing of this book, firearms account for approximately 19 percent of childhood deaths (ages 1–18).[2] Children are more likely to be killed by a gun than a car accident, suffocation, or poisoning. We must not allow this to be the status quo.

This book is about the big things that require collaboration and alignment across entire schools, even communities beyond their gates, but it's also about the little things that every single person can do to make the world a safer place. At least to make *your* world a safer place. If you find yourself without a list of tangible action items that you can implement by the end of the book, I've failed.

I grimace at the question "What's the one thing that would make schools safer?" There is no panacea. As we'll discuss in great detail, my fundamental belief is that everything in life is a calculated risk. Therefore, I cannot guarantee you will be safe. Instead, I work to educate you on the risks and the sensible mitigation tools with which you can improve your own chances of being safe. I know it's a burden and a great responsibility. You. Those around you. Your community. In that order. That's the flow, and that's how we'll prioritize safety.

If you're reading this book as an administrator of a school, I want you to get your pen and paper ready and build your action plan as we go. I've called out some action items that I think are the most universal, but many others are found buried in the stories we'll examine.

If you're reading this book as a parent of a child in a school, my greatest ask to you is to prioritize what you bring to your

[2]"Underlying Cause of Death, 2018–2021, Single Race Request," n.d., https://wonder.cdc.gov/ucd-icd10-expanded.html.

administrators. David Allen, a productivity expert, said so bluntly, "You can do anything, but not everything." This is as true of your children's school's administrators as it is for you. In this book are some of the tools to evaluate and prioritize risk. That's how you do the right things.

If you're reading this book as a teacher, a board member, or a member of a community at large, my hope is that you'll pay close attention to the roles and responsibilities outlined in Chapter 7. Those will guide you invariably toward the most successful possible outcome given a set of terrible facts you may have to wade through.

If you're reading this book in a crisis of your own, please reach out for support. You can reach me, or my team, you can reach your local teams of first responders, or you can reach out to a friend in education who may have a contact, but please don't go it alone. I am convinced this work takes a village. Preparing, responding, recovering, preventing, these are team efforts. The work will be hard. You deserve a team of supporters.

Acknowledgments

To the faculty and staff at the first schools I trained, you put me through a university of sorts, enabling me to learn how to build a business that would serve you and countless others. Thank you.

To Janet, who patiently and diligently sat with me for hours on end to describe the challenges her school was facing and test new ideas for how to solve them. Joffe Emergency Services exists today because of you. Thank you.

To Tom, who put the phone in my hand and said, "Sink or swim" as I made my first cold call. Without you, there would be no company.

To my mother, who lovingly and patiently, and patiently (see what I did there?), raised me. Without you, there would be no me.

To my colleagues at Joffe in both the early days and the more recent. There are too many to name specifically. Those who helped us get started never got to see the business thrive, and those who have seen it thrive will never know of some of the darkest days. Both groups have made this organization what it is. Thank you.

To the Advisory Board at Joffe, who challenges my thinking in every conceivable way. Thank you. With your partnership we are building something incredible.

To Rebecca and Ashley, my village, who helped to make writing this book possible.

To Scott, who got me started down the path of writing.

To Steve and Marilyn, who provided start-up money to a kid with no credit.

To the patients and students we've protected, you give us purpose.

To Lorena, you've created a light in the darkness. Thank you.

To Ed, who created the initial inspiration for my work in outside-the-box-EMS.

To Charlie, who brought context to my work.

There are countless others whom I wish I could identify specifically. As you'll read, my life has been touched by numerous incredibly generous relationships. I am forever grateful to be a part of this village.

To you, if you're reading this, thank you. I hope it helps. Please write to me at Chris@JoffeEmergencyServices.com with feedback, questions, and stories for the decades ahead.

Introduction

This is a book about people. It's about how we think, feel, and respond to some of the hardest moments of our lives. It's about what we can do to overcome the barriers that hold us back from taking action. It's about how we can work together to ensure every school is as safe as possible for the children who attend them. It's a book about emergencies, but more specifically, it's a book about the impact emergencies have on us as humans, and how we can prevent, prepare for, and mitigate the impacts of the emergencies that we'll inevitably face.

I wrote this book because I had a sudden realization during the early days of Covid that I am not a baker, I didn't like Tiger King, and I couldn't stand the idea of an air fryer. I, and my team, were actually as busy as we'd ever been during those first days working to help schools transition from in-person learning to virtual, to develop testing operations, and to craft plans for Covid exposures. I'm a school and event safety consultant and operate a nationwide school safety organization serving primarily K–12 schools in the US.

I realized during the pandemic that the work my team is doing in schools will, at best, reach tens of thousands of schools. We'll never be able to get to everyone. I believe every school deserves to have the tools to be as safe as possible, and I believe the lessons we teach can help every school get there. The goal of this book is to offer some of the tools and insights we have shared with tens of thousands of educators across the country so you can work with your team to implement them. From here, it's up to you to implement these strategies, and my sincere hope is that between the book and the accompanying online resources you will be able to do just that.

I've observed all too many school leaders, school communities, and even public safety leaders struggle through emergency response and recovery. In so many cases, I hear quite literally,

"There's no manual for enduring crisis." My hope is that you now have that manual; a tool to help you endure crises, and perhaps a tool to help you prevent them and mitigate their long-term implications.

There have been hundreds, if not thousands, of pieces of research done on the intersection of psychology, decision making, emergency response, recovery, and human connection. This book would not have been possible without the enormous body of work from which I'm building upon. I cite many experts and researchers throughout this book, but the body of work that existed before me is too vast to cite individually. At the end of this book are a list of other books, references, and materials which you might consider reading—many of these influenced my perspective.

Throughout this book, we talk about crisis and emergencies because that's what I've always been passionate about. And that's what you came here for. But at the heart of emergency response are the people responding to them. Their actions. Their emotions. Their thoughts. So I also spend a lot of time talking about that—the physiological and psychological components that define emergency response. The first part of this book is focused on this: the human aspect of emergencies. I share information about how our brains and bodies are programmed to respond in crisis, how we can manage that response to work in our favor, and how my personal interaction with crisis and trauma has shaped my perspective and understanding.

In the second part, we talk more about how humans tend to work together—and against one another—as they respond to crisis and how I've learned people can work together in crises the best. We discuss the importance of understanding and building relationships with students throughout your own community to increase meaningful, timely, and proactive communication. Finally, we'll discuss how to build teams that work together to respond to major crises.

In the third part, we unpack the school-based emergency using time as our guide for some of the critical items that need to happen. In medical training, we use the phrase "time is life" to convey the importance of quick hospital treatment for a stroke, a heart attack, or a traumatic incident. In truth the work we're talking about is no different. In emergencies, items not completed in the immediate will begrudge us throughout the rest of the process. We unpack the actions to take—and not to take—to make the best use of time along the continuum of an emergency.

The most disappointing truth I must confess to you is that there is no such thing as a 100 percent guarantee of safety. I wish I could say otherwise. As we will uncover, everything in life is a calculated risk: driving, flying, even loving. I believe *life* is selecting which risks are worth taking and that *intelligence* is managing the right risk along the way. I want to help you shine the light on the risks around you and help you mitigate those that are unreasonable or misaligned with your values.

Throughout this book, I use the word "I" quite a bit because my use of the word "we" might be confusing or create grammatical errors and issues. There is very little I've ever done alone that is worth writing about. While they're not named individually, I owe a debt of gratitude to my incredible team, our most collaborative and well engaged clients, and so many more partners from law enforcement, EMS, Fire, and other organizations. To protect privacy and out of respect for those involved, I've changed names and locations of most critical examples and events I mention throughout this book.

I recognize that living life day-to-day as if you're in a perpetual state of emergency is neither practicable nor reasonable. But as a starting point, it's important to know that being prepared for anything that could happen—anything that's conceivable in each instance—is essential for work, life, and one's pursuit of happiness. This is what this book is about: studying, preparing, and positioning yourself for the unexpected, including an occasional or incidental emergency. Let's get started.

I

The Crisis Experience

1

How We Experience Crises

What Is a Crisis?

When I say the word "crisis," what do you think of? Maybe you picture a person who is choking and needs their airway cleared. Or a flooding basement. Or an emergency evacuation due to nearby wildfires. There's no doubt that these are crises. But the truth is, crises come in all shapes and sizes. A missed deadline. A fender bender. A canceled flight. A broken arm. These are not usually what we think of when asked to imagine a crisis, but they can be powerful inducers of stress, and set off a physiological response that can mirror what we experience in a larger-scale crisis such as a school on fire or an active shooter event.

Dr. Saul McLeod defines stress as "a biological and psychological response experienced on encountering a threat that we feel we do not have the resources to deal with."[1] The body and brain have an automatic, programmed response when they detect stress. This means that we're practicing crisis management on a near daily basis. This is an important reminder to kick off this book, and for our understanding of how we, as people, respond to emergencies. Because it means you already have many of the tools we'll work to galvanize together.

I want to note that I'm using the word "crisis" here intentionally. Throughout this book, we talk a lot about emergencies, which we define as situations that have the potential to cause physical or emotional harm to a group of people. Here we're using the word "crisis" because we're referring not to the nature of the event itself but the stress response it triggers in individuals. Whether it's a burning building or a burnt dinner, our brains can see both as a crisis, depending on the circumstances, and both can trigger a stress response that impacts us physically, psychologically, and emotionally.

What happens to our brains and bodies in crisis?

Have you ever been on an airplane with more than a little turbulence? You likely have—perhaps many times—and you likely

---

[1] Saul McLeod, "What Is the Stress Response—Simply Psychology," 2010, https://www.simplypsychology.org/stress-biology.html.

know the feeling you get when it happens. Maybe your heart skips a beat when you're lifted out of your seat by one of the bigger bumps. Maybe your stomach is in knots. Maybe you feel a rush of anxiety as your mind races and envisions what might happen next. Maybe you go into planning mode—deciding what you'll do if something goes wrong and the plane has to make an emergency landing. Maybe you tell yourself, "I've been on a million flights before with turbulence; this is just like those. I'll be fine."

That's the human stress response. Every moment of every day, our bodies and brains are interpreting what's happening around us. With every experience we have and every situation we find ourselves in, our bodies are taking in information, putting the pieces together, assessing it, and deciding whether it's stressful. The decision is based on a combination of sensory input and processing (what did I see and hear in the situation?) and stored memories (what happened the last time I was in a similar situation?).[2] This information is sent to the amygdala, an area of the brain that contributes to emotional processing, which then interprets the images and sounds. If it determines there is danger, it instantly sends a distress signal to the hypothalamus, the part of the brain in charge of the stress response.

Here's what happens next:

> The hypothalamus operates as your body's "command center" (a term we'll use throughout the book to mean the center of decision making for the key stakeholders). Your brain communicates to the rest of your body via the nervous system, which controls your body's core functions such as breathing, heartbeat, your fight-or-flight response, and more. In essence, your nervous system can be further broken down into two sections:
> Your sympathetic nervous system: fight-or-flight response (think of the accelerator in your car); and
> Your parasympathetic nervous system: rest and digest (think of the brake pedal in your car).

---

[2]McLeod, "What Is the Stress Response—Simply Psychology."

When your hypothalamus (command center) sends a danger signal to your sympathetic nervous system, you go into what's commonly known as fight-or-flight mode, and your body begins to activate its response. On a school campus, this would be like telling all your security officers to brace for incoming danger. They'd run around and check every exit, stop releasing students from the buildings, "shunt" all the people they could into a specific part of campus and then work to defend that part of campus to the best of their ability while they wait for help. Well, your biological and physiological systems are doing the same thing. Your body begins shunting all available resources to your brain, heart, and core and begins using a stress hormone called cortisol to speed things up that need to go quickly. Your heart rate speeds up, your blood pressure goes up, your breathing gets faster, your sight, hearing, and other senses become more sensitive, all of which helps your body put on a better defense against the risk you're facing.

All these changes happen so quickly that you're not even cognitively able to process the event until after your body has processed and distributed some of these chemicals and fortified its defenses. It's truly incredible to reflect on all that our bodies are hardwired to do. Every so often we hear about a mother who lifts a car off her child or some other seemingly superhuman feat. This is thanks to the strength unlocked via your nervous system releasing epinephrine (adrenaline) and shifting blood glucose and other naturally occurring chemicals to your cells in order to accelerate and strengthen your defense mechanisms.

Similarly, every so often we hear about the person who jumped out of the way of an oncoming train. Same concept here. They probably didn't even realize what they were doing in the moment, but we are biologically hardwired to protect ourselves, and sometimes our biology takes over.

But these states are designed to be short-term. And your body will eventually require a recovery period to downshift from the crisis experience. We'll talk more about that in later parts of the book, but for now, I want to remind you that you're not superhuman, just human. That means you can do truly awesome things and you'll also be exhausted by them (that's the parasympathetic nervous system at play).[3]

How does this all apply to emergency response? Well, a lot. But the first thing is that the way we think, react, feel, and even move might look different in an emergency than it does in everyday life. Many times, people actually respond very differently from how they expected they might during an emergency response.

In *The Unthinkable*, Amanda Ripley's book on crisis and what enables some to survive when others don't, she deeply assesses the reality that our "disaster personalities can be quite different from the ones we expect to meet."[4] She shares what you might have even seen in your own behaviors: some people expect to be apoplectic during an emergency, yet they become the ideal leaders. Others, the opposite.

Knowing how our brain and body are reacting in a real-time crisis also helps us understand where to leverage our adrenaline-induced strengths and navigate the things that become harder when we're under stress. When we're in crisis, these are some of the things we can expect:

- When the amygdala takes control, adrenaline floods the brain, which allows us think faster;
- The parts of our brain that control rational thought are suppressed, which means we have increased anxiety and are quicker to act and react;
- Muscles get tense, and blood flow increases, which dilates our pupils to let in more light;
- Our breathing becomes shallow, which increases our heart rate and blood pressure;
- Our short-term memory is impaired, which makes it more challenging to handle social or intellectual tasks or behaviors;
- Pain is temporarily lessened.

---

[3]Harvard Health, "Understanding the Stress Response," July 6, 2020, https://www.health.harvard.edu/staying-healthy/understanding-the-stress-response.

[4]Amanda Ripley, *The Unthinkable: Who Survives When Disaster Strikes—and Why* (National Geographic Books, 2009).

As a result of these physiological changes, we tend to simplify messages. Under intense stress and possible information overload, we often miss the nuances of health and safety messages because we either aren't fully hearing information, can't remember the information, or are misinterpreting information we're receiving.[5]

We also look for additional information and opinions. We remember what we see and tend to believe what we've experienced. During crises, we want messages confirmed before acting. We often seek these out through looking for multiple channels or accounts reporting the same information, calling people we trust to find out if something is accurate, or looking to a credible leader. (There will be much more on leadership throughout the rest of this book.)

Finally, we experience fear. Obviously, crises can induce this, and the fear may be based in any number of concerns. How will this affect me? Could this hurt me? Could this hurt my child? Could this harm my reputation? Fear can be a limiting factor or an agent of progress, a catalyst for action. For the purposes of this conversation, we'll focus on the other elements/components of the crisis, but to explore fear more globally, you might pick up a copy of Gavin DeBecker's *The Gift of Fear*.

For a test of sorts on how you'll stress and potentially experience a crisis, you can go to IndigoPathway Career Survey and run a self-assessment to learn about who you are as a leader and as a contributor and see your stress reactions.

I often work with Sheri Smith, Founder and CEO of Indigo, to unpack and better define stress reactions for different personality types and some of the ways that people experience stress according to your DISC profile. Everyone is unique and this, too, is not designed to be a one-size-fits-all approach, per se, but this is at least a starting point for how you might be perceived and how you might behave. A quick introduction/refresher to the DISC personality assessment, initially created by psychologist William

---

[5]"CERC: Psychology of a Crisis," Centers for Disease Control, 2019, https:// emergency.cdc.gov/cerc/ppt/CERC_Psychology_of_a_Crisis.pdf.

Moulton, is that you're rated on a scale to assess which of these traits come out the most and which come out the least. In general, we can then categorize potential stressors and stress behaviors to paint an abstract picture of how one might behave.

D: Dominance
I: Influence
S: Steadiness
C: Conscientiousness

While there's much more to it, the basic premise is that using this self-assessment, you can conclude which of these personality traits come out higher or lower than average for you. Then, given the large body of data that exists, you can draw some conclusions about how you might handle a situation, manage stress, and so forth.

Like many leaders, I happen to be a High-D. This means that if I'm on your campus managing a crisis together with you, I'm likely going to be perceived as rushed, top-down, and judgmental, maybe even irritated. A reality is that in fact that's just my stress response. It's not personal, and it's seldom authentically how I'm feeling, but part of the way I stress outwardly is to move fast, move independently, and manage a large volume of information quickly. What's important about that realization is it enables me to prepare my team. Because I now know this, they do, too! And, by the end of this book, I hope to help your team better understand who you are as a leader so that together, you and your team can achieve greater success in navigating inevitably difficult discussions and situations. Take a moment at the end of this chapter to examine your DISC persona and then to evaluate how you *stress*. From there, you can do this same exercise with your full leadership team and command center. You'll work better together for the discussions that will ensue.

Action item: Go to the accompanying website and take the DISC assessment and focus on your stress reactions. Come back to the site to look at how you might stress differently than others in your community.

Stretch goal: Conduct this assessment with your entire leadership team and use it to determine how you'll work best together during crises.

Your stress behaviors from your DISC assessment combined with your human realities will provide an interesting—again, abstract at best—image of how you might behave during crisis. Let's take a moment to reflect on those human realities in the same way. In general, humans have one of these three reactions to a crisis, sometimes more than one.

A combination of these physiological and psychological stress responses can leave leaders in a difficult position at the start of a crisis:

Fight or Flight: Activation of fight-or-flight response: most common during an imminently life-threatening emergency. Fight or flight is the biological response caused by the soaring epinephrine (adrenaline) and cortisol (stress hormone) released at the beginning of a crisis. You're biologically programmed to survive, and your body's response is designed around giving you the best of your energy and senses and will automatically deprioritize things such as remembering whether you need to use the restroom or if you're hungry.

Analysis Paralysis: Analysis paralysis commonly occurs during creeping crises that emerge over days or weeks. It is the psychological or social emotional response that often plagues leaders at the beginning of the crisis. It's also known as "freeze" in a more acute situation (you might have heard the phrase "Fight, flight, or freeze"). It's the inability or unwillingness to move forward for fear there might be another option and/or because one is too consumed by choices, too overwhelmed to even consider progress.

Denial: Denial is frequently experienced along with the stimulus of the initial event and sometimes is replaced by one of the responses above. Anecdotally, I can share that denial is the place that most people start out in a school based emergency.

It's refusing to believe that something happening is true or refusing to believe that the magnitude of that very event is as significant as it is. I posit that denial poses the greatest risk to our communities because denial costs us time. If you don't acknowledge the emergency, you won't be responding to it. Therefore, much of this book is designed around managing denial. This is the subject of the next chapter.

2

Finding Solid Ground When Crisis Emerges

"When you choose to view your stress response as helpful, you create the biology of courage."
— *Kelly McGonigal*[1]

Stress in our day-to-day lives can become a chronic problem. As we just discussed, heart rate, blood pressure, breathing rate all go up, and our vessels constrict. This is great news when we're facing danger and need to manage it in a time-bound situation. Evolutionarily, this was useful in case we were attacked by a lion, for example. In modern times, it works well when we're in a car accident, fighting off an assailant, or when the meal we're cooking suddenly catches fire. But if left unregulated, it'll eventually cause severe problems.

I introduced the concept of denial in the previous chapter, but it's such a central challenge in emergency response that I want to explore it further. Denial, because it costs us time, is among the greatest risks during an emergency. I worked with a school with students who are deaf or hard of hearing. They use American Sign Language to communicate between faculty, staff, and students. I was observing a drill when one student, in an act of defiance, covered his eyes as his teacher was explaining what to do. He couldn't hear, so by covering his eyes, he was activating his denial (albeit also his defiance) mechanisms. I see leaders, community members, and so many others essentially cover their eyes or deny that an event is unfolding—or as we'll identify in the risk section, that an event *could* happen.

I live in Santa Monica, California, and in 2022, there was a plane crash on the beach.[2] It was a harrowing situation. At about 3:30 p.m., a pilot and a passenger took off in a single-engine

[1]Kelly McGonigal, "How to Make Stress Your Friend," Presentation, TED.com, https://www.ted.com/talks/kelly_mcgonigal_how_to_make_stress_your_friend/comments.

[2]Gregory Yee, "Cessna Airplane Flips in Crash Landing on Santa Monica Beach," *Los Angeles Times*, December 23, 2022, https://www.latimes.com/california/story/2022-12-22/santa-monica-beach-cessna-plane-crash.

airplane from Santa Monica Airport and flew up to about 3,000 feet and turned "right" (or north) to fly toward Malibu. Evidently, the engine of the plane began to experience some trouble, so the pilot radioed Santa Monica Tower and said, "We need to turn back." Santa Monica Tower radioed back and said, "Are you having an emergency?" and the pilot said "no." About eight minutes later, the pilot radioed back again and said "emergency. . .I'm going to need to put it down on the beach," implying he didn't have the engine power to get back to the airport and would need to land the airplane on the beach. He managed to get the plane on the ground, though unfortunately, his passenger had a heart attack and didn't make it.

A frustrating reality of many of the stories I share throughout this book is we will seldom know what *could have happened*. It would be foolish of me to say that had the pilot declared an emergency at the beginning, he could have gotten what he needed so that he didn't land on the beach but instead, at the airport. One could argue that if that had occurred, the passenger may not have had a heart attack. But I don't have a crystal ball, nor can I change the past. So instead, I take everything we can learn from the story as it was and leave it at that. In my work, I've come across thousands of people who made split-second, life-or-death decisions. The only thing they have in common is that I normally meet them afterward. Put differently, I've only ever met the ones who survived. Given that, it simply wouldn't be right to Monday-morning quarterback the decisions of those who didn't. I will do the best I can to articulate learnings for you and your community so that you have the best chance to endure whatever the event might be.

So, back to the beach. Well, there are some interesting opportunities to opine on this situation for the purpose of learning. I'll start with the pilot:

> "Are you having an emergency?" There's been an upswelling in pilots being encouraged to use the phrase "Priority handling" instead of "Emergency" with the theory that in order to have an emergency, the pilot probably screwed

something up. Given that, it's a hit to the ego and self-identity to declare an emergency, and pilots *might* try to avoid it. I see this as one of the greatest examples of denial. For a pilot in crisis, there is *no* better solution than to call ATC and have them get planes the hell out of your way and help you find a place to land, but at times, ego, or machismo[3] (as the FAA defines it as one of the 5 Hazardous Attitudes), or some other nonsense gets in our way.

This, though, isn't a book about pilots and airplanes, it's a book about schools and leaders, so let's take some different examples:

- Could a fire ever destroy your campus?
- Could a teacher ever be arrested on campus?
- Could an employee of yours ever sexually assault a child?
- Could an active shooter event ever occur on your campus?
- Could an earthquake ever impact your school?
- Could a global pandemic ever shut you down?

If your answer was "no" to *any* single one of these questions, you just experienced denial. I need you to keep reading. Objectively, these things are possible. Horrific, awful, painful experiences, in some cases, but suggesting that they "could not" happen is simply denial. If you answered "yes" to all these questions and subsequently had a stress reaction, you, my friend, are my people. Objectively, of course any of these things could happen (even earthquakes in places that don't frequently experience them as we'll talk about later on). Humans are capable of some of the most incredible things: we build relationships, we build families, we have the propensity for deep and meaningful love, connection, and impact; but humans are also capable of the very things we see on the news that we work so hard to mitigate.

---

[3]Federal Aviation Administration. "Chapter 2: Aeronautical Decision-Making," n.d. https://www.faa.gov/regulationspolicies/handbooksmanuals/aviation/phak/chapter-2-aeronautical-decision-making.

The good news is that there are some tools that we can give you, right now, that will help you manage the human response that elicits denial.

The first of these tools is to default to progress. Default to progress is a decision we make today to take action, to risk being wrong or overreacting, but to define our steps in the first seven seconds of an emergency. It's a commitment to moving forward even if we're in denial. It's a combination of mindset and training at its core. In fact, it's a commitment I want you to make today: **Rather than vacillate on whether this is real or imagined, rather than negotiate denial vs acceptance vs action, that we see the risk and we act on it as though it is real, and allow our brains and psychological defense mechanisms time to process as we're physically acting.**

Reverend Dr. Martin Luther King, Jr., said, "If you can't fly then run, if you can't run then walk, if you can't walk then crawl, but whatever you do you have to keep moving forward."[4] This, at its core, represents the concept of default to progress. We can— and we must—always keep moving forward. Even if the steps are small ones, they are steps in the right direction.

Let's put it into practice: You hear something that sounds like gunshots. Instead of analyzing and assessing whether that's a gunshot, a car backfiring, or someone who slammed a door down the hall, you take action and initiate the lockdown response or the active shooter response you've been trained on. You make the call to act before the incident escalates, and in doing so, when it does happen, you get yourself and your students into a position of safety that much more quickly.

Let's keep going: You're in a crowded place and start to feel the crowd pushing and begin to wonder if you'll be able to get out. You escape now. You don't wait to find out that you can't.

[4] "'Keep Moving from This Mountain,' Address at Spelman College on 10 April 1960," The Martin Luther King, Jr., Research and Education Institute, May 24, 2021, https://kinginstitute.stanford.edu/king-papers/documents/keep-moving-mountain-address-spelman-college-10-april-1960#fn1.

You move diagonally against the current and work your way to the sides of the crowd until you can self-extricate.

As a pilot, your plane has engine trouble. You don't want to see if it gets worse, you don't check more things, you declare an emergency and get to the ground so that you can figure it out there.

In some of these cases a choice to default to progress will inherently mean you overreact. It might be a door slamming, a crowd who just really loves Taylor Swift, or a fluke with the airplane's engine, but you don't wait to find those things out because time is your greatest tool in the emergency response equation. In non-emergencies, we're taught to critically think, often, even to slow down, assess more facts, bring in experts to consult with. Emergencies, though, call on us to have a specific—and different—approach. Responses are most successful if we've done that thinking already and we work with the outcomes that we've previously established.

A note about overreacting: We're in a world where people are often scared. We operate with an increased level of anxiety. I don't take it lightly to say that we should run the risk of overreacting. I realize that can compound the global anxiety and create a traumatic stress reaction for people, which can also do damage. In my work, though, I've learned we must prioritize the things that will hurt you the most imminently and severely, and we prioritize in that way. Said differently, if you don't react and it turns out to be an active shooter, not a door slamming, the consequences could be huge. If you do react, and it turns out not to be an emergency, there may be consequences but you've survived.

I've made a choice. One that I hope you will make, too: I'd rather overreact multiple times and be wrong than to underreact even once and lose a life.

Analysis paralysis. This is, in some ways, what default progress is here to combat. In and of itself, analysis paralysis can be a manifestation of denial. I encourage people in trainings and real-life situations to run this play:

1. Acknowledge the "thing" is happening. Say it out loud if you're struggling, simplify it, if there's time. Acknowledge it.
2. Commit to the concept that there is only one reasonable choice, and that is to act.
3. Act based on what is within (y)our control.

So, using the loud "bang":

1. "I hear what might be gunshots."
2. "Given that, I'm going to take the action that I should if there are gunshots around me. We're going to activate our lockdown response."

This is a (life?) lesson that we can take with us to overcome not just the life-threatening emergencies we face but the critical decisions in life.

Practice Makes Permanent—Tool # 2

If you grew up hearing the phrase "practice makes perfect" repeatedly, the idea of "practice makes permanent" might sound a little. . .different. While it might be true that practice can make perfect for a musician or an artist, what we're talking about here isn't playing the cello; it's building habitual responses to emergencies. It's the permanence of information and creating a type of "muscle memory" that dictates your reaction in a campus emergency. (Side note: I never became perfect at playing the cello, either.)

Brain science comes into play here, too. Practicing, anything for that matter, creates new connections between the neurons in your brain; those connections become pathways for information to travel in the future.

To take this out of emergencies for a moment, did you play the piano as a child? Or learn a language in school? You may not be very good at it these days if you haven't kept your practice up, but you may be able to pick it back up more easily than you realize because those pathways haven't gone away, they've just gotten a little unkempt. Picking up the piano or traveling to a country where they speak that language you used to know would help you retread those pathways.

Practice makes permanent means we become what we practice. It changes our brain, how we see the world, and what we can do. The challenge for communities then becomes that we need to combine practice with continuous improvement. (Which, by the way, your school has already finely tuned when it comes to curriculum!)

The Importance of Emergency Drills

Our goal is to practice enough through emergency drills that we reach what we often think of as "muscle memory"—where our response is automatic and we don't have to try to remember the steps to take when in the crisis moment. This allows us to continue to progress even when faced with the psychological and physiological symptoms of stress. It allows us to make the choice today to default to progress such that when we're faced with a crisis, we don't have to wonder what steps to take, vacillate on whether it's real or perceived, or take any other actions that might delay our response.

> **Action item:** At least once per month,* conduct a drill to practice the knowledge.
> **Check your local laws to ensure you're doing drills at the right cadence for your age groups served.**

You'll want to create a series of traditional training sessions for staff and students to experience on a routine basis. My teachers always said repetition was important for learning. I hated math and I desperately wanted to stop that repetition, but they wouldn't let me, citing decades of learning in the space about how important repetition was. This is true for emergency preparedness, too. You should be conducting at least one drill per month to practice especially those first few seconds—and minutes—of an emergency before help or meaningful, directive communication can begin. Your drills should be focused on creating confidence and increasing people's capacity to quickly make the choice to act and to go through the processes they will need to use for real emergencies. This is the most effective way to build muscle memory so that if cortisol levels are high, our bodies can take over for us. Practice makes permanent.

What's the difference between a good drill and a bad drill? A good drill:

- Is successful because people were challenged, but to a level at which they could still succeed. It builds muscle memory *and* confidence.
- Clearly identifies that it's a drill (more on that in a moment).
- Involves all people who might normally be on campus (it's not at 7 a.m. when only half of your community is there).
- Leverages multiple "wrinkles" or "injects"[5] to not just do the same thing repeatedly.
- Offers live feedback along the way helping people understand if they've made a mistake and how to course correct.
- Has a recap at the end. Our trauma-informed practices teach us that we need to reflect in order to remain psychologically safe.
- Generates learning through practice *and* data presented back to the community.
- Builds on the last one's successes, scaffolding learning and confidence.

---

[5]*Inject: to introduce as an element or factor in or into some situation or subject.* "Definition of Inject." In *Merriam-Webster Dictionary*, February 25, 2023. https://www.merriam-webster.com/dictionary/inject.

Time the drills and try to improve throughout the year:

- Awareness to execution: Especially for lockdown/active-shooter drills, how long did it take to go from announcement or catalyst to the desired outcome?
- Hold time: If you're doing lockdown drills, how long did you hold people in lockdown?
- Evacuation time: How long did it take to "dump the building" or evacuate all people from the building?
- Command center activation time: How long did it take to establish leadership/incident command?
- Attendance time: How long did it take to take attendance and account for all students, staff, visitors, vendors, and parents?
- Debrief time: How long did it take to do a quick debrief with everyone?
- Total time: How long did the total drill take? You should expect variations from drill to drill (e.g. lockdown drills always take longer because you'll have two phases, the lockdown and the release vs the evacuation drill where you only have a release). But in general, you can expect drills to get slightly faster as the year goes on with a few exceptions we'll talk about in Chapter 10.

Use this list to challenge yourself and your community and reflect on whether you're doing good drills. On the accompanying website, there's a practical handout that you can use, and this is repeated there to help you ask the right questions and ensure you're doing good drills.

Philosophically, though, here's the most important takeaway: In September, your students are the youngest they'll be all year, your teachers may not know all students quite yet, and you may have a big portion of new people on campus. Your youngest grade and your newest teachers, not to mention others who may have transferred, don't know your protocols at all. Given this, you're probably doing a straightforward drill without a lot of "wrinkles" peppered in. However, as you go through the year, you should be building up toward a full-scale/Moulage Drill (we talk about that in Chapter 10) to ensure that you can endure not just the first seconds, but the entire process all the way to reuniting children with their families.

What's a bad drill?

Fundamentally, a bad drill is the opposite of everything we've just talked about.

A bad drill:

- Generates no learning.
- Challenges people beyond the point that they can be successful and leaves them feeling like they've failed.
- Has sensorial items (simulated gunshots, simulated injuries, or other similar simulations, which the community isn't ready for).
    - Note: If the community is ready for these, there can be a time or place for some sensorial items, but if you watch the news, you've seen at least a few of these played out terribly—often with good intention but terrible and painfully traumatic outcomes. Please consult with a child psychologist, an adult psychologist, and multiple external experts before conducting a sensorial drill.
- Lacks a clear beginning, middle, and end.
- Lacks a debrief or any data reflection.

My favorite saying is that **an imperfect drill is a perfect opportunity to learn.** A bad drill doesn't mean that there were mistakes. A bad drill means that we as a community did not learn from those mistakes in a way that was trauma-informed. We'll define trauma-informed much more rigorously in Chapter 4, but in short, it's a recognition that trauma is more common than previously thought and we run the risk of retraumatizing people. Given that, we must seek to work in a way that is aware of that potential trauma and explicitly focus on not retraumatizing our community.

It's critical that we don't just teach and practice but that we regularly assess our progress.

We've got to answer tough questions such as:

- How are we improving year over year?
- How are we adapting to changing world circumstances? (Read: Have we updated our risk assessment to ensure we're planning for the right risks and concerns?)
- How are we building confidence in our community, and have we tested situations such as their performance without the key incident commander/leader in place?
- Have people taken appropriate action in their first seven seconds routinely, or are we struggling to get people to default to progress?

These assessment questions are critical to continuous improvement and will lead back into the teaching phase. We should be taking our assessment questions and asking ourselves how the next year's teaching can inform and enhance our responses.

Time Value of Life

Are you familiar with the basic concept of time value of money? If not, a quick refresher/introduction to it: The basic premise is that a dollar today is worth more than a dollar tomorrow because you can invest the dollar today and earn something back on it and so a dollar tomorrow is just a dollar, whereas today's dollar invested could be $2 tomorrow. Never mind the fact that we just earned a 100% return on our dollar. My retirement planner would be thrilled.

The time value of life is a concept I introduce here to help you contemplate the value of drills, practice, and investing time and money into safety and security work.

It goes the same way. An action taken at the catalyst of the emergency is worth more—in life safety—than an action taken 10 seconds later. An action taken 10 seconds later is still worth more than an action taken 10 minutes later. The faster people do the right things, the less risk is left unchecked and the more people, generally, whom we can protect—or save.

TIME VALUE OF LIFE

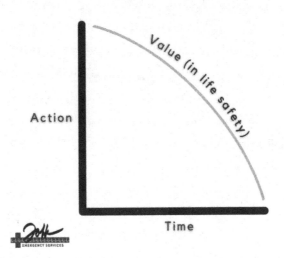

In emergencies, time is life and training is insurance.
We'll work through both at great length in the chapters ahead.

3

My Experience
with Crisis

People often ask me why I chose to go into crisis management. The truth is, in a strange way, crisis has always felt like home to me. I had a unique upbringing, which included some very hard and destabilizing experiences, and some extraordinarily lucky twists of fate, both of which solidified a few things for me. First, that life is fragile, and children are uniquely vulnerable to its fragility. And second, people are amazingly resilient.

I was born in St Louis, Missouri, and don't have full clarity on where, when, or how. It's an unusual way to explain an origin story, I know, but I was the fifth child of a sex worker, so the paperwork from my early years is scant, as are my memories. I was removed from the home I was born into before my first birthday, taken from every family member I had ever known and placed in the foster care system. Some of my biological siblings were also eventually removed (I later learned) for neglect and child abuse.

After being separated from my biological mother, I lived in an orphanage for a short time and a series of temporary homes with foster families. This included one foster home where a child died from neglect while I was living in the house. My first two years of life were highly unstable. They were painful. They were traumatic. And they had lasting effects on me, in ways I know and likely in ways I don't.

At two years old, something incredible happened that changed my life completely. I was adopted by my mother. At the time, my mother was a young, single woman seeking to start a family. She was (and still is) a warm and affectionate woman, and she dedicated herself to being a parent—my parent. Growing up, many of my friends had good parents, but there was always something different about my mom. She wasn't just a good mom; she was a great one. She knew how to parent through remarkably dark and hard days. She shared my history of adoption with me so young that I don't ever remember not knowing that I was adopted. Often people refer to her as my "adoptive mom," which to me signals a qualifier that is wholly inappropriate. She's my mom.

My mother patiently and lovingly raised me and my sibling. She opened her home, her arms, and her heart to us, and to this day I feel enormous gratitude that we were lucky enough to have found each other. I truly feel like I hit the jackpot the day she decided to take me home. Everything I have, and everything I will ever have, is because I was adopted by my mother.

Following my adoption, my life became much more stable, and I had a fairly normal set of early life experiences. I made friends. I played in the snow. I went to school. I enjoyed the life I had in Missouri with my new family, followed by a new life in California after we moved to Los Angeles when I was four/five years old.

But it didn't take long before I had a series of experiences that reminded me how fragile life is. These were experiences that impacted me, some very directly and some more subtly or subconsciously. But each gave me a new perspective—slightly shifting the lens through which I saw life and personal safety. And each became a formative experience that solidified my commitment to making the world a safer place, particularly for children. Here are some of the stories and lessons that have shaped my perspective.

A Shaken Sense of Safety

The first time I remember coming face-to-face with questions about safety was in 1999, when a family friend, Jonathan, was the victim of gun violence. I was nine years old at the time, and Jonathan, a close family friend, was six. On the morning of August 10 of that year, an armed assailant walked into the Jewish Community Center in Granada Hills and shot six people, one fatally. Jonathan was shot in the ankle and hospitalized, and fortunately recovered from his injuries, but the experience left scars for those present that day and those connected to them, too.

After Jonathan was released from the hospital, I remember talking with him and asking if it hurt, if he was scared, if he thought he would die. More than two decades later, I don't fully remember his exact answers to my questions, but what I do remember—what was imprinted on my memory from that conversation—was an understanding that Jonathan's sense of safety would be forever changed. I remember being incensed about how unfair it was that Jonathan would now go back to a familiar place—a community and childcare center, a place that was supposed to be safe—and now he would be scared. I wondered what it would be like if I were in that position, and what I could do to help him or others who felt that way.

Loss, Confusion, and Grief

Less than a year later, I had another experience that left me confused and angry. I was working over the summer at the early childhood center my mom ran in California. A boy named Michael was one of hundreds of preschoolers who attended daycare at the center, and I got to know him. I spent hours that summer playing on the playground with Michael and the other preschoolers. I have vivid memories of pushing Michael around in the fire truck on the blacktop, driving him in circles, switching between helping him go faster and trying to get him to slow down.

That fall, the day after back-to-school night, my mom sat me down to share some news. Michael, she told me, had passed away suddenly the night before. Michael had choked on a piece of chicken cartilage and he didn't make it. I didn't understand how it was possible for something like this to happen. My nine-year-old brain kept asking questions. How could a piece of chicken kill someone? How could someone so young die? Could I die? Isn't there something we can do? I desperately tried to make sense of it, but I couldn't.

Tackling the Paralysis of Fear

When I was 17, I witnessed an accident that changed how I understood emergency response. During a stint working with horses, I was working in a barn when a woman was thrown from a horse. I didn't know her personally, but she had been riding the horse around the barns when it got spooked. The horse bucked, reared, and kicked violently. Eventually, she fell to the ground. Hard. I was near where she fell and could hear her body being thrown from the horse and hitting the ground. I remember that sound, even today. And I remember the moments after as the horse ran off and she laid there, motionless. My mind scrambled to figure out what I could do, how I could help. I didn't have any training at the time, and I had very little exposure to these types of medical events, so I didn't see many options. Somebody else called 911, and I stood there, frozen. I felt utterly powerless.

A few months later, partially propelled by what I had experienced in the barn, I made the decision to become an EMT. It was a career path that felt right for me at the time: a place where I could tackle some of the questions I had been pondering for a decade and take some action to make the world a little less scary for myself and others. I got hired that summer and began responding to 911 calls in Southern California.

I was still in training when I got one of my first big calls: a bus vs. wheelchair. I arrived on the scene, and it was clear that the person in the wheelchair was in trouble. I began performing CPR. It was my first time administering CPR on a real patient, and despite my many hours of training and practice, I was plagued with insecurity and self-doubt. I remember asking myself: *Am I supposed to count chest compressions out loud, or is that something we only do in training? Is this movement in her chest good, or am I doing something incorrectly that's making things worse?*

I remember telling myself that I had been trained for this and was reassured that a trainer was watching me, helping me, and ensuring that I was doing the right things. I remember being terrified and telling myself to focus on just what comes next. One step, even a small step, would be a step forward.

Seeing My Trauma in a New Light

The summer I graduated from high school (just as I was becoming an EMT), I recruited three of my friends to drive across the country with me to St. Louis. I had a plan to go meet my birth mom for the first time since being adopted. I had been searching for answers around what my life might have been like had things worked out differently—about what would have happened if I had stayed with my biological family. I had hired a private investigator to track down my biological mom, and he gave me three possible addresses.

My friends and I piled into the car, armed with a carload of snacks and drove straight through for 36 hours to St. Louis. We'd gotten in late, so two of the guys slept in while my friend Jared and I went to the first house on the list. We knocked on the door and found ourselves face-to-face with a woman. Pretending to be a rep from the power company, I asked, "Are you Patricia?" She said yes. I took a moment, and then told her I was her son. I'll never forget her looking at me, or the mental gymnastics that I could see her doing—and I'm sure I was doing, too—as we realized this connection that we shared.

I spent the day with her, learning about her life, my biological family, and what my life would have been like had I not been adopted. I learned that my other siblings had, in large part, not been able to attend school, let alone college. One of them had been killed, and some of the others were struggling. I saw and fully realized how the stability my mom provided me had transformed my life.

Learning about my early childhood also helped me understand myself in new ways. A childhood therapist had noted at one point that one of my coping mechanisms was being "hyper-vigilant"—remaining always on guard, on edge, awaiting the next destabilizing event. I have always been excessively prepared for things to go sideways. I have always been hard to startle. And I have regularly found myself assuming the worst in other people's intentions and actions. These have been challenging attributes at times, hurdles I have needed to overcome, particularly in the context of relationships. But that day, learning more about my original family and recalling the trauma I experienced helped me contextualize these qualities and started me on my path toward seeing how these qualities could become a strength to help others navigate through trauma and crisis.

The Challenges We Collectively Have Yet to Overcome

On the day after Christmas in 2020, I had another pivotal experience that influenced my perspective again. This time, it was clear to me that there are still enormous hurdles that keep us as a society from doing our best for each other. I was in the middle of a run when I noticed a woman, visibly shaken, standing at a bus stop looking at something in a nearby tree. I could vaguely see the tree from where I was running, so I got closer. As I did, I realized it was a person, a man about my age, motionless and suspended from the tree with a sweatshirt that had been fastened as a noose around his neck.

I decided to act. After all, I now had the training and experience I had lacked in the barn more than a decade earlier. I turned to the woman and asked if she had called 911. (I hadn't brought my cell phone on my run that day.) She said she hadn't, and she said, yelled, actually, "I'm scared, and I'm waiting for the bus." I pleaded with the woman to call, even anonymously, but she refused.

Seconds later, the bus arrived, and as soon as the doors opened, I ran onto it. For context, I'm mid-run, still shirtless, and a sweaty mess. I said to the bus driver, "I need you to call 911, and I need your first aid kit." He said no. In fact, he said, "Get off my bus." I made it clear to him that there was a medical emergency and described the situation to him and then reiterated what I needed from him. But the bus driver turned around to me and just said, "Get off my bus, or I'm calling the police." And I said, "Please do. I need help. I need you to look over, and I need you to see that there is somebody who is in that tree and that we need to help him." And the bus driver said again, "Get off my bus," as he started to motion to close the doors. I realized that if I didn't get off now, he was going to start driving (ironically, given how counter that was to his instruction to me). If he kept driving, this man wasn't going to get any help.

So I got off the bus and ran back to the tree where this man was hanging. I went to the tree and began untying the knot that the makeshift noose was tied from in order to get him down. I saw another runner approaching, just as I was getting the first of two knots untied. I yelled to that runner, *"Please help! I need your help."* He looked, panicked and kept running, calling the police as he ran away. He shared some expletives, which I'll spare you from, but it is interesting to note that his reaction was actually probably more normal than mine. I was able to get the man down and finally called 911 from my Apple watch (something I had forgotten was a possibility up until that moment). I began CPR just as the fire department showed up. The fire department treated the man to try to resuscitate him but after a while, it was determined that the man was no longer going to be able to be saved. He was pronounced dead at the scene.

Years later, this experience still haunts me. Rounding a corner to see a man hanging from a tree is something no one should ever experience, but equally disturbing was the reception I got when asking for help. I certainly understand experiencing fear, denial, trauma, and paralysis in an event like this, but we can—and we *must*—find a way to overcome it when someone's life is at stake. We must work together in these moments, even if all we achieve is incremental progress, because safety is built on incremental progress. It's a flywheel. Each action opens new opportunities for progress that further improve the circumstances.

This experience taught me about the importance of committing up front, today, to act—even if I don't have all the answers. I may get it wrong, but my decision is rooted in the idea that I would rather try to help 100 times and fail each time, than not try to help even once and learn after the fact that my help might have made the difference.

We Are More Alike than We Are Different

Each of these stories has contributed to how I see the world. The combination is what propelled me to dedicate myself and my work to helping people be safe, feel safe, respond effectively, and recover collectively. Something in these pages, in my story, may have spoken to you, or mirrored something you've experienced at some point in your life. Maybe it was the trauma, the grief, or the powerlessness I've felt at times. Or maybe it was the optimism you aligned with, which seems to have made itself a permanent fixture in my worldview. Or maybe still it was something completely different. Regardless, I hope these helped you see where there might be points of alignment in my story with yours. Because despite the uniqueness of each of our stories, there are very few things in this world that we don't share in common with others. We have far more in common than in contrast.

You may have surmised by now that a big focus of this book—a big focus of my life and my work, really—is connection and relationships. This in large part because I believe wholeheartedly that connection is central to emergency response. Connection sparks action, facilitates communication, and empowers leaders and teams to respond effectively. It also helps people absorb information more effectively, in turn enabling more appropriate and time-bound responses.

This is also because I have always had an unrelenting belief that what ties us together makes us stronger. I've seen this borne out time and again in emergency response situations—from hospitals to schools to large-scale events. When we understand each other's perspective, supporting each other, listening to each other, and moving forward together comes much more easily. So now that you understand what has driven my story, let's keep moving forward—together.

II What All Emergencies Have in Common

4

The Common Threads of Emergency Response

In this chapter, I explore the concentric circles of safety and how they help prepare us for anything.

The first few minutes of every emergency are different, but the response, from about minute seven forward, is the same almost every time. Sometimes in emergency settings and in emergency training we oversimplify things. It's very possible that is what I'm doing here, but I hope to argue and explore this together through a framework that I refer to as the **concentric circles of emergency response**. Let's first describe and define what these circles look like, and then we'll further explore this idea through the lens of a few different emergencies.

Emergency managers describe the phases of emergency management with four (sometimes five) stages (Figure 4.1):

1. Mitigation;
2. Preparedness;
3. Response;
4. Recovery;
5. Prevention (depends on whom you ask; sometimes this is bucketed elsewhere).

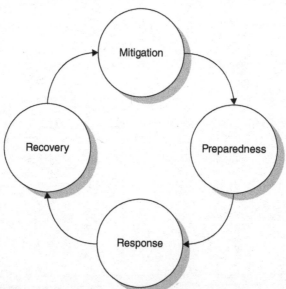

Figure 4.1: FEMA's Concentric Circles of Emergency Response.[1]

[1]Adapted from *Four Phases of Emergency Management: Emergency Management in the United States*, Unit Four, FEMA.

The significance of the cycle is that all communities are in at least one phase of emergency management at all times, and it's possible that a community might be in one phase from one emergency while adding an additional phase from yet another concern. For example, while the US was battling the pandemic, we also saw hurricanes, fires, and events of community unrest leaving some cities responding to multiple emergencies and working to mitigate or prevent others. One of the Heads of School I work with has said "we know one crisis is over because a new one has begun."

The concentric circles we've constructed should overlay these phases as an opportunity to move through a checklist of sorts as we're navigating each phase. In many cases, you can run this checklist over and over again and get a different result because you'll have a different set of circumstances at the beginning of an emergency than one hour later (Figure 4.2).

The checklist is:

1. Physical Safety:
   a. For you;
   b. For those around you;
   c. For those over whom you might have some influence or control.
2. Psychological Safety;
3. Communication;
4. Leadership.

Figure 4.2: Concentric Circles of School Safety.

Physical Safety

Fundamentally, the concentric circles begin with physical safety—the basic concept that before anything else occurs during an emergency response, the first and most important action that matters is getting *yourself* to a position of physical safety.

When you get on an airplane, they go through the opening talk of, "Put your seatbelts on. This is how it works." Typically, it's a terribly produced video or a set of flight attendants leading the demonstration. Eventually, they get to this place where they say, "If there's a loss of cabin pressure, you should put your own mask on before helping others." The idea here is that if there's a loss of cabin pressure, in a matter of seconds, you are going to lose the ability to function. Why? Because you will only have a limited amount of oxygen, and your body can't function without oxygen. The mask will give you the oxygen you need, but you have to put it on as quickly as possible to avoid losing consciousness before you get there. And therefore, you've got to put your own mask on before you can help other people.

It might surprise you, but even the professionals have this expectation. In emergency medical services (EMS), there is a phrase that is used to describe this concept: "BSI for my buddy and I." BSI stands for "body substance isolation" (gloves, goggles, and all the other stuff you might need to keep yourself safe from things that might go squirting or spraying around). You're first supposed to do that for yourself, and then you're supposed to do a buddy check and make sure that your partner or anybody else on your team has that stuff as well.

CPR training includes this concept as well. If you're a CPR-trained individual, you may be familiar with the phrase "Scene safety and personal protective equipment (PPE)," which again, references the need to make sure that the scene is safe before you act.

Across all groups of individuals ranging from police to soldiers, from firefighters to paramedics, from teachers to principals, even students, the very first and most critical thing we can do is to get ourselves to a position of safety. **And that argument is clear: If you're not safe, you won't be able to help anybody else.**

In order to be of value to the emergency response as a whole, we first have to be of value to ourselves. We first have to make sure that we get ourselves into a position of physical safety. The first circle—the center point of our concentric circles of safety—is, therefore, physical safety.

Psychological Safety

The next circle is psychological safety. I would argue that this has been undervalued or underrepresented pre-COVID-19, at least in the disaster education space. I won't speak for other areas, but I can say that as it relates to emergency management in education, we have perseverated on physical safety, working to answer the question: How do I make sure that people are physically safe? And we've undervalued the importance of psychological safety in the emergency response, recovery phase, and in the preparedness phase. We've undervalued the inextricably linked question: How do I make sure people feel safe? I posit that we cannot answer one or the other alone but must ask them sequentially. First, how do we get safe? Second, how do we feel safe?

Psychological safety, as I'm referring to it, is also different than the way your own psychologist would define it. Bear with me here because the times that we're working on are transient, inherently fraught with trauma and easiest to assess in the rearview mirror. Psychological safety, in the concentric circles, refers to doing as much as is appropriate to communicate, set expectations, and hold space for the fact that we're in a challenging situation. That definition will change depending on the type of emergency and the circumstances, but there are some basics that should be in place for every emergency:

1. Have we communicated enough information to the people surrounding us?
2. Are we withholding information because we want to or because we need to (required by law, investigative purposes, etc.) or simply because we don't have it? Have we told people that?

3. Have we created space for expression? Can we do so?
4. Are we listening to our counselors? Can we do so?

Obviously, the first moments of an active shooter event are not the time to listen to our counselors, but this is a time where we might benefit from them having reviewed our strategy in advance. We'll unpack this further as we explore how it changes as we move through the emergency response. It's critical to note that at this point, psychological safety is a consideration, a central one, but execution is going to look different at every moment of the response and recovery.

> **Action Item:** Schedule a meeting with your counselors or mental health resources to review your emergency plans and drill strategy to ensure that you're acting in a way that honors potential historical trauma in your community.

Psychological safety needs to be accounted for in all phases of the emergency management cycle: preparedness, response, recovery, and mitigation. Psychological safety does not just begin after the emergency. In so many cases, as soon as the emergency happens, we bring in the grief and crisis counselors. We need to bring those crisis counselors in—or at least their philosophies, structures, and systems—as part of a trauma-informed preparedness strategy and response strategy.

Often, when we describe something, we also find our own minds wandering around what it's not. Here's an example: In many cases, well-meaning folks have established lockdown drills that are as realistic as possible, including shooting blanks from a gun in order to "help people identify the sound of gunshots" or having a masked intruder run through campus banging on doors. I believe that highly sensorialized lockdown drills with K–12 students are largely misguided. There is a better way.

I understand there may be some communities, cultures, even countries, that value these approaches. If this fits into your norm, I won't challenge that without considering your unique circumstances. In my experience in the United States, in general, there's a better way. In fact, I'll describe that better way as we work our way through the book.

Psychological safety is violently upended when it comes to these drills. There was a particularly notable incident in Indiana where the local police department lined teachers up and shot them with pellet guns in the back of the head, or neck, or back, "execution style," in order to have them feel what it felt like to be shot.[2] Teachers walked out of that session feeling psychologically unsafe. They had created a traumatic event, and then they had asked people to come back and engage in that space in a healthy, wholesome, educational way. For some people, that was possible, but for many, it was not. "They told us, 'This is what happens if you just cower and do nothing,'" one teacher told *IndyStar*, which did not name the teachers. "They shot all of us across our backs. I was hit four times. . . . It hurt so bad," one teacher said in an interview. This type of experience raises our stress hormones and cortisol levels, creating an environment in which we simply can't learn.

In the drill I just mentioned, a psychologist could have identified that creating a trauma-inducing experience would actually be counterproductive from a teaching and learning perspective. Had a psychologist been engaged, they may have encouraged the school's leadership to seek out different ways of meeting the goals and objectives of the drill.

There's a body of work referred to as trauma-informed care, which builds upon the premise that traumatic experiences are common in society. Trauma-informed care calls on us to not repeat these experiences and, in whatever ways possible, to restore a sense of safety, power, and self-worth.[3] There are some

---

[2]Carla Herreria Russo, "Teachers Reportedly Shot 'Execution Style' with Pellets in Active Shooter Drill," HuffPost, March 25, 2019, https://www.huffpost.com/entry/teachers-shot-active-shooter-drill_n_5c93fc99e4b0a6329e142b5a.

[3]Substance Abuse and Mental Health Services Administration. "SAMHSA's Concept of Trauma and Guidance for a Trauma-Informed Approach." HHS Publication No. (SMA) 14-4884. Rockville, MD: Substance Abuse and Mental Health Services Administration, 2014.

critical principles fundamental to a trauma-informed approach (Figure 4.3). These include:

- Safety;[4]
- Trustworthiness and transparency;
- Peer support;
- Collaboration and mutuality;
- Empowerment, voice, and choice;
- Cultural, historical, and gender issues.

These concepts are not only central to designing a healthy school environment but, more importantly for our shared purposes, are also critical in contemplating an emergency preparedness

Guiding Principles of Trauma-informed Care
SAMHSA's Concept of Trauma and guidance for a Trauma-Informed Approach

SAFETY	Faculty, staff, students, and families feel physically and psychologically safe.
TRUSTWORTHINESS & TRANSPARENCY	Organizational operations and decisions are conducted with transparency and with the goal of building and maintaining trust among faculty, staff, students, and their families.
PEER SUPPORT	A key vehicle for building trust and establishing safety and empowerment among faculty, staff, students, and their families.
COLLABORATION & MUTUALITY	The organization recognizes that everyone has a role to play in a trauma-informed approach and that healing happens in relationships and in the meaningful sharing of power and decision-making.
EMPOWERMENT VOICE & CHOICE	The organization aims to strengthen the faculty, staff, student, and families' experience of choice and recognizes that every person's experience is unique and requires an individualized approach.
CULTURAL, HISTORICAL & GENDER ISSUES	The organization actively moves past cultural stereotypes and biases, offers culturally responsive services, leverages the healing value of traditional cultural connections, and recognizes and addresses historical trauma.

Figure 4.3: SAMHSA's Guiding Principles of Trauma-informed Care.

---

[4]Substance Abuse and Mental Health Services Administration. SAMHSA's Concept of Trauma and Guidance for a Trauma-Informed Approach. HHS Publication No. (SMA) 14-4884. Rockville, MD: Substance Abuse and Mental Health Services Administration, 2014.

program. Without psychological safety, we'll have stress, and in stress, as we've defined, we'll have physiological stress responses, which will impede our ability to learn, engage, and lead. At their worst, stress responses will block our ability to take action, leaving us vulnerable and potentially less safe.

Communication

The third circle is communication. When we think about communication, often we think about the post-crisis communication. We're thinking about how we are going to reestablish our school community. How we are going to rebuild our structures and our systems. How we are going to ensure that we re-instill a sense of confidence in staff, faculty, students, and parents. How we are going to ensure that we reestablish our financial stability or resiliency (emergencies tend to be expensive).

I've been a part of thousands of emergencies, either as a responder myself, working to debrief afterward, or counseling a school or venue through the recovery process. I've seldom seen a large-scale emergency handled by the professionals—police, fire, EMS, etc.—nor by an individual school where communication wasn't an opportunity for improvement. Further, note that when two organizations come together—when the police plus the school are working together or the fire department plus the school are working together—it's even less common to see communication come up as an area of strength. This is further exacerbated expotentially by multiple external agencies, for example in the DC area, where there are multiple law enforcement agencies working with a single school.

This isn't all bad news; there's a methodology in emergency management/response for multi-agency responses, meaning responses where multiple different agencies (police, fire, EMS, schools, etc.) come together. It's called the Incident Command System (ICS), and I describe this in much greater detail in Chapter 7. By the time we're finished with this book, you'll have a framework that will help you at least construct the skeleton of good communication. From there, you'll have to practice to make it permanent!

Communication is one of few parts of the emergency that families will see (and therefore critique). It's also among the parts of the emergency and its response that are memorialized for history to reevaluate over time. Communication is the bedrock for leadership; without communication, leadership fails. Great communication enables an emergency recovery to be done more quickly because it leverages the tenets of trauma-informed care, defines next steps, and demonstrates empathy all throughout the message. For all those reasons, I see many leaders struggle with wordsmithing, and it's a place where analysis paralysis emerges.

The good news is that knowing this and focusing on it can, rather easily, turn communication from a deficiency into a strength.

Leadership

The last circle is leadership. When I use the term "leadership," you may think of superintendents, heads of schools, principals, or CEOs. There are certainly times and places where those people are critical as the leaders of the response, but leadership morphs at different moments of the crisis. In the first moments of an emergency, every single adult on campus needs to be capable of taking leadership for themselves and for those in their immediate vicinity.

The goal is to ensure that in order, we've created a sense of physical safety, psychological safety, effective communication, and then move into a place focused on leadership.

One of my colleagues, a head of school, introduced me to the idea that school is fundamentally a set of pillars: people, place, and program. People to teach and people to learn, space to do the same, and program or curriculum with which you do the teaching. Like Maslow's hierarchy of needs, though, only once we've established those four baseline elements (physical safety, psychological safety, communication, and leadership) do we get and have the ability to run the people, place, and program of the school.

Often people also ask, "What happens if you get to physical safety, then psychological safety, then communication, then leadership, and then the emergency isn't over yet?" This isn't just an isolated situation. Maybe this is a lockdown, where things are evolving quickly, and yes, we might have done those things and gotten to a place of physical safety by getting into a lockdown, getting into a classroom, or an office, or a closet, or some space on campus. We got to a sense of psychological safety by trying to work through our stress management and do what we could to contain the situation in the moment. We worked on communication by letting people know what was going on. We worked on leadership by somebody taking charge and becoming the incident commander. But the emergency is not over yet. We rerun this cycle. Are we physically safe? Can we improve psychological safety through something as basic as communication (if it's safe to do so, whispering or playing a card game)? These things shift with the urgency and severity of the emergency, but that's the point! If your incident commander has given you more information by now, you get to start to adjust your behaviors, and the whole community can be better off for it.

What's wonderful about this framework is that we get to keep going using the same framework repeatedly. This framework applies to the preparedness, the response, and the recovery elements of emergency response in schools. In a few chapters, we'll uncover the use of the framework using the "rule of 7s (sevens)." Covering the items accomplished and left outstanding in the seven seconds, minutes, hours, days, weeks, months, and years after the catalyst or the emergency itself, we'll leverage these four steps, repeatedly throughout those "7s." Once we've established the first four—once we've established physical safety, psychological safety, communication, and leadership—we focus on people, place, and program, and then we get to start that process again.

So when I say the first few minutes are different, what I really mean is the catalyst for the emergency is going to be different. In practice, the response is going to be the same. Yes, I realize that in an earthquake situation, the way that we will get physically safe is to drop, cover, and hold; in a lockdown situation, the way that we'll get physically safe is to get behind a closed and locked door; in a tsunami situation, the way that we'll get physically safe is to get to higher ground.

So even though the mechanism through which we will achieve physical safety will look different, the concentric circles are going to be identical, at the very least in schools.

As we start to approach emergency training this way, we should also be working to convey the *why* behind dropping, covering, and holding. It turns out, in US schools, it's less about the building collapsing (that's possible, but unlikely) but instead about the risks we're facing from things on the wall, ceilings, etc. We convey the reason behind the tactics that we're asking our teachers, our students, and our leaders to use so that as they move through the process, they understand why they're doing it and without any effort, they automatically remember, "Put my mask on before somebody else." They're instantly remembering why they need to put their mask on; that's our goal, and that's what we try to do in every training. This is what we should all be trying to do in every training and experience that we provide for faculty, staff, and students.

What's the Point?

Early in my career, I was working at a major trauma center. I was in the radio room and ran out for a quick bite to eat when I heard the public address system go off and call out level-one trauma inbound—seven minutes away. I headed back to the trauma bay to get to work. As I got back, I began the process of setting up. First, I had to put on a gown in case blood was sprayed at any point. Then, gloves so that I could touch the patient and do whatever was necessary to support treatment. Then, glasses. Again, sometimes "blood happens" during these treatments. The bells went off again, and I heard, "Inbound five minutes."

At this point I'm no longer alone in the room. There are at least 30 other people who are in and around the room ready to receive this patient when they arrive. As usual, we're chatting, talking about who's going to do what, and working through the different scenarios that we might expect. It's gotten loud because there are so many people in the space. So loud in fact that at times we can't hear one another speak. Because of our quick movement at times people are also getting pushed near and far. The bells go off again. ETA two minutes. At this point I can hear the sirens in the distance, and they're getting louder. The trauma surgeon walks around the corner.

And in a very quiet and small way, he commands our attention. He says, "I want this to go smoothly, and I want people to listen to one another. One voice at a time. One step at a time. That's what will give our patient the best opportunity."

Sure enough, we listened. The sirens shut off, the hospital doors opened, and the patient was wheeled in. Without having been told any of this, the paramedics handing off the patient were also quieter, more collected, and better organized because that is the environment they walked into. They gave report, we accepted the patient, and we began treatment, one voice and one step at a time. Indeed, the patient had a better outcome as a result of the organized, methodical, strategic, and high-quality communication approach that we took to treatment.

I share this because, in my work today, I respond to schools during emergencies. I no longer have lights and sirens, and this means that I arrive somewhere between 30 minutes to 24 hours after the emergency has begun. Often, I respond to a wild fire that has burned near or on campus or a student fight that has escalated and caused serious injury. Other times, I respond to a small fire that has taken place in the building or in some cases even an individual with a weapon on a school campus. This is by no means an exhaustive list but reflects some of the most stressful situations for our school leaders to manage through.

So when you're facing an emergency on campus, one of the things I often challenge school leaders to do is to channel their inner-trauma surgeon, and:

1. Sit down;
2. Get some water;

3. Speak with one voice at a time;
4. Communicate the way we traditionally do.

There's no one definition of what makes a good crisis leader. As I think about nonmedical crisis leaders and crisis leadership, Brené Brown's philosophy comes to mind. As Brown has observed in her work and describes in great detail in *Dare to Lead*, the best leaders tend to be people who are vulnerable. It's interesting, but those who are terrified to get things wrong are often the worst crisis leaders.

I suppose you could put it differently and say that ineffective leaders tend to be people who are not as willing to be vulnerable in each moment. I've observed that people who are willing to be vulnerable during a crisis are generally willing to be vulnerable consistently otherwise.

The ones who are more willing to lean into their vulnerability—which is Brown's philosophy—seem to be able to tap into self-awareness and use the insight as a catalyst for growth and progress. Those who are more attuned to the fact that they're vulnerable tend to do better in crisis.

So, in fact, all emergencies—no matter where they start, no matter how big they are, and no matter how long their effects might be felt—boil down to communication and leadership. And you can't get to those elements without physical and psychological safety.

5

Analyzing Risk

Everything in life is a calculated risk. Driving, flying, walking, learning, loving. Living, fundamentally, means choosing the risks you're willing to take. I wholeheartedly believe that life is fundamentally weighing the pros against the cons, thinking through the causes and effects and the consequences that come along with the risks we take.

There's a reality that by taking on the responsibility of leading a school, you have to incorporate the management of risks you're willing to take into your day-to-day leadership. You can't just say, "Well, there could be an active shooter, but I'm not going to worry about it." Vulnerable leadership means you also probably wouldn't say, "There could be an active shooter, so I'm going to close the school forever." The tension between these concepts, the polarity that exists between risks we are tolerant of vs. those we're not willing to accept is different in every community. That said, there's a framework that you can use to at least organize your leadership team's perspective around risks. It's widely adopted and likely represents something you've seen used in financial risk analysis.

The basic formula for risk assessment is:

$$Likelihood \times Severity = Risk$$

Sometimes you can control the likelihood, other times, you can control the severity, and sometimes, you can't control either. We'll get to a place of comfort with all of this as we continue.

The way to interpret this formula is concrete and universal. An actuary somewhere at your insurance company could tell you the statistical likelihood of a lightning strike on your playground, a car accident in your drop-off line, or an active shooter on your campus. For the purposes of this book and your entrée into risk management, I don't want or need you to become an actuary. I need you to become an approximate-ary. (Please forgive that dad joke).

Importantly, you have to be vulnerable in the risk identification process. Vulnerability, in this case, may be the antidote to denial.

Only when you acknowledge that there are risks you don't want to contemplate can you prepare for them. That preparedness will ultimately protect lives.

The likelihood side of the equation is exactly what it sounds like—the likelihood that something will happen. That's based on a number of factors such as geography, topography, community makeup, ages served, historic events, rules, barriers, and countless more. To put some of those variables into context, if you have a gas station next door to your building, you're more **likely** to have a fuel leak than to run out of fuel for your generator. Similarly, if you have had an incident occur on your campus before, you know it's possible. Hopefully you've done work to mitigate the impact, but you know it's possible. If your school backs up to the woods, you're more likely to have a bear on campus than if your school was on the 10th floor of a high rise in Manhattan. It's not impossible just because you're in Manhattan, but bears don't generally know how to take the elevators . . .

You're evaluating the likelihood of something happening and then the likelihood of something happening in your community vs. some other school. That's the hardest part of the equation. In general, here's a list of variables that affect your likelihood side of the equation, which you can use to inform your dialogue:

A starting list of variables affecting likelihood:

- Geographic Risks:
  - What are the natural disasters possible in our area?
  - What are the natural disasters possible on our continent that might have geopolitical, resource, or other impacts on our more localized region?
- Neighborhood Risks:
  - What is the makeup of our more immediate surroundings? How do those affect us? Banks in the area increase the likelihood, for example, of a bank robbery, creating an on-campus concern.

- What is the general risk level of our neighborhood?
  - People:
    - Crime;
    - Sex offenders.
  - Property/other:
    - Types of structures vs. wildland;
    - Access management (how many streets get to and from our school)?
  - Mitigation opportunities:
    - Closest fire/police stations.
- Community risks:
  - Age of students served;
  - Playground equipment.
- Obviously, this is a partial list, but hopefully it's enough to motivate you to visit the accompanying website (scan the QR code in the back of the book) and dig deeper into the various risk factors that we can study in order to mitigate and/or inform the responses we might need.

Action Item: Visit the accompanying website to challenge your thinking and explore a broader list of potential risks you might face in your community.

The second half of the equation is severity. In this half, our question shifts to: "How severe are the consequences if **that** something happens?" Let's use those same two examples. If there's a fuel leak, that could be severe. If we think about the potential outcomes of a leak and think about the potential for an explosion, which could be significant, we then realize we need to get an expert (a local firefighter who oversees the area might be enough) to help us interpret the risk we face from that eventuality. By contrast, thinking about a child who might fall, if there's a broken arm, that could be highly severe for that student but is likely not a severe event for the community.

That second reality ties in an important part of the severity variable. When we assess severity, we're assessing it on behalf of the community. At Joffe, we've created a four-part methodology to assess community impact and base our assessment on the impact to people, property, environment, and reputation. Environment can be broken down further into literal, digital, or social/environmental consequences, and depending on the risk factor we're discussing, I like to pick one or more of the three (literal, digital, or social/environmental) to evaluate against.

Obviously, a hacker is going to pose danger to the digital environment, but it's important to then think about whether they might have the ability to lock down the building, which could cause damage to our physical environment if we needed to break down doors in order to free trapped students.

- People: Might it hurt or kill someone?
- Property: Might it damage or destroy property?
- Environment (physical): Might it cause damage or destruction to our physical environment?
- Environment (digital): Might it cause damage or destruction to our digital environment?
- Environment (social): Might it cause damage or destruction to our social environment?
- Reputation: Might it cause damage or destruction to our reputation?

The goal of this risk assessment process is to prioritize your risk. It's neither practical nor desirable to eliminate every single potential risk (that goes back to the start of the chapter—we have to select which risks we're willing to bear). But we do need to work through a process to determine which risks are most likely and most severe, and this equation and chart are a useful tool to do so (Figure 5.1). Once you know your most likely and most severe risks, then we can move to the next step, which is to determine how to mitigate them.

The basic formula for risk mitigation is:

$$Preparedness \times Notification = Mitigation$$

People	Property	Environment	Reputation	Scale	Unlikely to occur in industry or geography (1)	Has occurred rarely in industry or geography (2)	May occur with no provocation in industry or geography (3)	Reasonable probability it will occur in industry or geography (4)	Likely to occur in industry or geography (5)
No injuries	No damage	No impact	No effect	0					
Slight injury	Slight damage	Slight impact	Slight effect	1					
Minor injury	Minor damage	Minor impact	Limited effect	2					
Major injury	Local damage	Local impact	Considerable impact	3					
Single fatality	Regional/major damage	Regional impact	Major regional/national impact	4					
Multiple fatalities	Extensive damage	Massive impact	Major national/international impact	5					

Severity — As defined by consequences for:

Probability

Figure 5.1: Risk Assessment Matrix.

This is a less mutually agreed-upon formula. Said differently, I didn't make it up, but it's not nearly as well adopted as the risk formula above is. The idea here, though, is to tackle the formula from left to right with a series of questions to assess the mitigation strategies that are necessary.

Can we prepare? If so, to what degree? If we're concerned about an earthquake, there are structural preparedness activities, related preparedness efforts, and training-related preparedness efforts that we can undergo. The beauty is that those things will not change the likelihood of the event, but they will absolutely reduce the severity of the impact. Reinforcing buildings, for example, will make it less likely that the buildings will topple. Building an annual process where we ensure bookshelves and furniture are secured to the walls will help us ensure that we've accounted for the risk of falling debris, and so forth.

Similarly, notification is an interesting concept to mitigate damage. The further in advance we're notified of something, the more we can do to manage around it and thus reduce severity. If, for example, we're notified an earthquake is coming (something we now can know about up to one minute before it strikes), we can get into earthquake position—drop, cover, and hold on—and are much more likely to establish a position of safety that can reduce the severity of the damage to people. Similarly, if we only get 10 seconds notice, we have a lower likelihood of getting the message distributed effectively and may not get to take advantage of the mitigation of notification. This is all to say that as you're prioritizing, it can be helpful to also run through the mitigation formula and for an event like a pandemic, which you'll generally have days to weeks of notice about, worry less in the moment about physical safety than perhaps an active shooter, where you're likely to have little to no warning. You should still get to your pandemic plan because it's going to be severe and reasonably likely, but you should prioritize your active shooter plan. Why? You'd have less notice, preparedness is generally more in your control (because it's on your campus), and more importantly,

RECOMMENDED ACTIONS
Manage/monitor for progress into increased risk categories
Develop focused teams to mitigate/ maintain awareness of risk
Incorporate risk-reducing and response measures
Eliminate risk if possible, community-wide focus if not

Figure 5.2: Recommended actions.

measuring by the four pillars (people, property, environment, and reputation), your severity is likely higher.

Naturally, then, you need a key for all of this. Here's the answer key that I use (Figure 5.2):

In short, if the incident is high likelihood and high severity, we need to work to eliminate the risk if practical (trim the brush around us to increase our defensible space for a fire, build a behavioral threat assessment team to assess students for risk of harm, etc.) and/or reduce the consequences through training the entire community on what to do should the given event occur.

Conversely, if the event is low likelihood and low severity, we shouldn't drop it from our awareness, but we can prioritize the higher severity/likelihood items first.

Let's put it into action:

> Scenario 1: You have monkey bars on campus. Your risk of broken arms with monkey bars is generally higher than if you didn't have monkey bars on campus.

Your conclusion for your risk assessment for your monkey bars might look something like this:

Risk: Broken arms or physical injury on monkey bars.
Likelihood (you can use Red/Yellow/Green scale or 1–5):

- Red (without supervision);
- Yellow (with supervision).

Severity:

- People: Yellow (one child could break an arm, but it's highly unlikely it'll affect everyone on campus);
- Property: Green (really not much risk to property);
- Environment: Green (really not much risk to environment no matter how you define it);
- Reputation: Greenish (there's very little reputation damage if you have one incident. If you have 83, you'll probably be suffering some PR concerns).

That's it! Now, you can go to the next phase and start to think about your mitigation strategy. It might look like this:

We believe monkey bars pose an acceptable risk of injury. The benefits of improving reading skills (tracking, etc.) are evident and outweigh the risk of a physical injury. However, we will work to mitigate the risk to the fullest extent possible by:

1. Always have monkey bar play supervised;
2. Always limit monkey bar play to one student at a time;
3. Never let students climb on top of the monkey bars; we'll only allow them to be used as intended.

It doesn't have to be this detailed for every risk, but when you start to identify reds on the chart, you will want to have some defined statements like this to manage your training, emergency planning, and recovery efforts.

Your goal should be to reassess risk at least once per year or any time a major development occurs in the world (e.g. a world war, a global pandemic, a new weapon such as ghost guns is introduced). As a general rule, I recommend having your own risk assessment audited by an external party roughly once every three to five years. Ideally, you'd have an interdisciplinary party conduct the external audit (your insurance company, a safety consultant, etc.). A free and easy option is to have your police department audit every other year and then your fire department audit on alternating years to get the different perspectives that ultimately create the interdisciplinary kaleidoscope you're trying to look through.

6 Preventing Crisis through Relationships

"The more healthy relationships a child has, the more likely he will be to recover from trauma and thrive. Relationships are the agents of change, and the most powerful therapy is human love."[1]

As I alluded to in Chapter 3, I had an incredibly tumultuous early life. I was (and still am) a black man, out of the foster system, and raised predominantly by a single mother. The statistics on my proclivity for violence, high school graduation, and entrepreneurship are high, low, and abysmal, respectively. And I've struggled with self-sabotage and been incapable of self-regulation at times as I was growing up the data never tells the whole story though.

I'm often asked what changed the course of my life and enabled me to become a successful contributor to the world. I can tell you that I searched for years in therapy for the answer to that question, and in the end, I've concluded that it was the quantity and quality of relationships with an enormous number of incredibly and authentically kind, caring, and engaged people: people who took the time to get to know me and build my trust—teachers, coaches, horse trainers, horse-shoers, ranchers, the woman at the local burger shop (which I visit far too often according to my cholesterol levels).

Despite the odds, I never became a violent person myself, and I credit that to the relationships I was given the opportunity to hold. Someone—actually, quite a few someones—created connection for me, and I plan to spend the rest of my life working to help others find connection, too.

Relationships are often key to preventing crises. Realistically, they're **the** key to preventing crisis when the crisis is perpetrated by someone at the school or in the extended school community. If it's not, or if it's a different kind of crisis such as a natural disaster, relationships won't prevent it, but they can help mitigate

[1]Bruce D. Perry, *The Boy Who Was Raised as a Dog: And Other Stories from a Child Psychiatrist's Notebook*, 2007, https://openlibrary.org/books/OL17210964M/The_boy_who_was_raised_as_a_dog. / Hachette UK.

it, because established trust will make people move faster and feel safer in responding to emergencies. And there are ways to strengthen relationships systematically to identify threats and risks early and intervene.

Organizationally, the biggest impact you can create, in terms of both preventing and preparing for an active shooter or violent, school-based worst-case scenario, is a relationship between each student and an adult on campus and in the greater community.

In the early days of COVID-19, the public health world shared this analogy that each mitigation tool, masks, vaccinations, social distancing, and so on, was a layer of Swiss cheese. This was initially created by James Reason in 2000 to explain the occurrence of system failures and articulate the importance of successive layers of barriers, defenses, and safeguards. Alone, each item was porous, but together, they become less so. You can see an image I've used countless times in presentations in Figure 6.1. All emergencies have some basic elements of this. It's not just about the individual layer of mitigation, it's about a confluence of layers that work together to prevent the event and ideally to mitigate the event's severity.

Another version, adapted to account for active shooter– and/or active assailant–type situations, appears in Figure 6.2.

To take it a step further, think of every single adult-student relationship as an individual layer of Swiss cheese that is preventing that student from crisis or shaping the way in which that crisis might manifest. What's more? That Swiss cheese has a dual purpose: Not only does it work to prevent that student from experiencing their own crisis, but it also creates an opportunity to listen and hear your community, meaning that if something is brewing, students have a trusted adult with whom they can share that concern. Building this trust not only allows you to identify and intervene in potentially explosive situations, but it also can act as a pressure release valve for the student, who may have been struggling to connect with adults or peers.

In 2019, the US Secret Service National Threat Assessment Center, NTAC, delivered a report that concluded 83 percent of attackers shared verbal, written, visual, or video communications

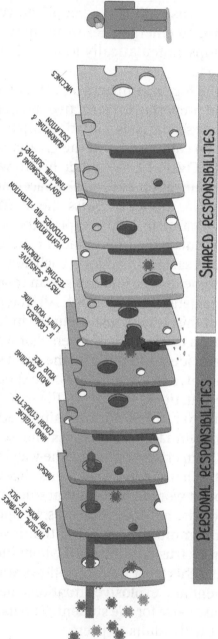

Figure 6.1: The Swiss cheese respirator virus pandemic defense.[2]

[2]Adapted from Mackay, Ian M. (2020), "The Swiss Cheese Respiratory Virus Defense," figshare Figure, https://doi.org/10.6084/m9.figshare.13082618.v26.

The Swiss Cheese Model of School Safety

Factors
FAVORING
Protection
• Education
• Community Trust
• Financial Support
• Harm Reduction
• Effective Risk
• Communication

Factors
UNDERMINING
Protection
• Misinformation
• Conspiracy
• Inequities
• Crisis Fatigue
• Hesitancy

Security
Strategy

Emergency Response
Practice (drills)

Emergency
Response
Training

Threat
Assessment
Team

Visitor
Management
System

Emergency
Notification
System

Incident Commander
with
succession plans

Reunification
Training

Board Risk
Management Committee

Safety
Committee

Violence Risk
Assessment Strategy

Cameras &
Monitoring

Campus Monitoring
Strategy

Anonymous Tip
Strategy

Reunification
Practice

Figure 6.2: The Swiss cheese model for school safety.

that indicated their intent to carry out an attack, threatened the target, and/or threatened others.[3] This specific dataset was relatively small (n = 29), but we've seen this hold true across multiple studies and multiple datasets. People don't just snap. With time, thorough and proper investigation and assessment, and a realistic network of folks the assailant interacted with, police and investigators have always been able to find a person or in many cases a few people who knew that the assailant was potentially dangerous.

When we look more broadly at the available data on school shootings and talk with survivors and those who've experienced them, there's a trend that's present. There are a few different ways that this data is parsed, but one statistic from the FBI's Pre-Attack Behaviors of Active Shooters in US in 2000–2013 concluded that on average, each shooter displayed four to five concerning behaviors over time that were observable to others around the shooter.[4]

So, if these attackers told someone and showed these behaviors in advance, why didn't we catch them before they caused harm? **You'd never know what the puzzle looked like if you only had one piece.**

Developing meaningful connections, then, becomes a defense mechanism for our schools, not just to prevent an active shooter. In fact, often when we conduct a behavioral threat assessment, we discover the student (the potential attacker) is experiencing trauma of their own and there is an opportunity to support them and prevent the attack, instead of being saddled with its consequences. That said, behavioral threat assessments are contingent

---

[3]U.S. Secret Service National Threat Assessment Center (NTAC), "PROTECTING AMERICA'S SCHOOLS: A U.S. SECRET SERVICE ANALYSIS OF TARGETED SCHOOL VIOLENCE," U.S. Department of Homeland Security, United States Secret Service, 2019, https://www.secretservice.gov/sites/default/files/2020-04/Protecting_Americas_Schools.pdf.

[4]Federal Bureau of Investigation, "A Study of Pre-Attack Behaviors of Active Shooters in the United States Between 2000 and 2013," November 15, 2018, https://www.fbi.gov/file-repository/pre-attack-behaviors-of-active-shooters-in-us-2000-2013.pdf/view.

on a catalyst. It'd be impractical to conduct them every day on every student. Instead, we need a community that's willing to come forward to identify a concern and share that concern with the threat assessment team. We need a community that's willing to say something when they see something, and we need leaders to know what to do. Those bouts of willingness are themselves catalyzed by strong relationships of trust, connection, and commitment carried out on a routine basis.

The report from NTAC highlights that there's a range of time frames within which an attacker conveyed their intent. This ranged from two weeks to one hour before the attack, and of the population NTAC assessed, they concluded that one third communicated their intent (via verbal, written, or digital dissemination) within an hour of the attack. This is key because the lesson this unearths is that we can't just have a see-something-say-something policy. We also must optimize that process for speed. I often use the language "They've said something; now we have to do something" as we work on building out these systems. The challenge can be once a threat or report is received, figuring out who on campus needs to get it and then what that person must do with it.

To give you a starting point:

1. If there's an imminent threat to people or property, call 911.
2. Get the information to the incident commander or the threat assessment team (or both).
3. Those folks must have a police connection or someone else they can rely on to help process the information and make the appropriate decisions.

Across the events I've worked or studied, in each case, there's been a distinct lack of connection in those environments, which tends to cause a troubled person to go unnoticed and spawn a plot without the opportunity for a check-in or a chance to resolve whatever is being experienced as a problem. Mind you, there may be other answers. But the lack of connection between them is undeniable.

Worse, when we look at these events in hindsight, it's seldom a surprise to those who were closest. This pushes us into a difficult conversation with implications far beyond this chapter. To keep us focused, I'll posit this:

> *In the vast majority of school shootings we've seen in the United States, if one person or agency had known each of the many details that so many people knew individually, I believe we could have stopped entirely or mitigated the damage from nearly every event.*

I'm not saying that people got it wrong. I'm saying we've historically lacked the systems, the fidelity to the systems we have, and the leadership and communication in this space to truly get to the bottom of what a person might be experiencing—or planning.

To put this into perspective, imagine I gave you one puzzle piece. Just one. I didn't tell you about it, but I told you it was important. Putting that puzzle together would change the world. You might seek out others whom I might have given another puzzle piece to, right? You might build a team, even, to look for where the puzzle pieces were. The great problem we're running into is that searching for those puzzle pieces can be hard when we don't know who has them. That's the challenge we have to be solving for.

Then, to make matters more complicated, as Richard McNally puts it: "Although mass murderers often do exhibit bizarre behavior, most people who exhibit bizarre behavior do not commit mass murder."[5] Yeah, you read that right. Now, you've got puzzle pieces, and you've started to put them together, and the third of an image you can see is blurred by the reality that not everything is as it appears.

---

[5]Richard J. McNally, "Why Psychiatrists Can't Predict Mass Murderers," Salon, January 12, 2011, https://www.salon.com/2011/01/12/jared_loughner_mass_murderers_diagnose/.

We can't get it right 100 percent of the time. I often reframe the dialogue to increase the number of students on our collective radar. To do this, we assess students who sustain any life change (divorce, death in the family, even a behavioral or grade change at school). We constantly evaluate the quality and quantity of relationships and recognize when one is shifting. And, in high schools, that happens a lot.

Our goal is to intersect the security teams with the health teams with the admin teams on a campus and ensure that we're constantly facilitating the assembly of a puzzle. Most of the time, the puzzle leads to a typical student, but we get the opportunity to apply care, support, and added engagement for those students and enable them to feel support and to engage their connections.

The gaps between puzzle pieces can lead to an alarming lack of resilience in a troubled student. Missing out on building the puzzle pieces means missing out on understanding the full picture, or the full burden, a student might be carrying. One of the most significant ingredients for resilience is simply having adults in your corner—someone who is meaningfully engaged with the student in some basic, daily way—a campus mental health professional, security officer, nurse, teacher, custodian, or administrator. We can all be that person. In fact, we are all probably already that person for someone—it's up to us to ensure that we keep showing up.

7

Organizing Teams, People, and Resources to Respond

We have examined how we, as humans, react and respond to emergencies, we've explored the common elements of every emergency response, discussed how we analyze and assess risk to prepare to keep our communities safe, and delved into the importance of building and maintaining relationships to prevent and mitigate crises. Next, we'll look at a framework to organize teams, people, communication, resources, and information in emergencies. It's called the Incident Command System (ICS), and it's been an invaluable tool for crisis response for schools—and other organizations—around the globe. In all emergencies, we find leadership and communication are the challenge, and the ICS model helps to establish a successful framework for each of those.

Incident Command System

The Incident Command System was developed in the 1970s, by a group called the Firefighting Resources of Southern California Organized for Potential Emergencies, FIRESCOPE, as part of an effort to better manage wildland firefighting.

There were two problems that they were trying to solve. The first was this idea that if multiple agencies would respond to a single wildfire, it would be unclear who was in charge. At best this could lead to confusion and wasted resources. At worst, this could actually exacerbate the danger by creating crossed lines of communication. The FIRESCOPE team aspired to create a system that was flexible enough to be used by a single fire department to respond to a wildfire effectively and one that could also be used to coordinate multiple agencies responding to the same fire.

To put the value of ICS into context, in the United States, we have 27,189 different fire agencies,[1] 18,000 different police agencies,[2]

---

[1]Kahn, Laura H., and Jeremiah A. Barondess, "Preparing for Disaster: Response Matrices in the USA and UK," *Journal of Urban Health-Bulletin of the New York Academy of Medicine* 85, no. 6 (August 28, 2008): 910–22, https://doi.org/10.1007/s11524-008-9310-y.

[2]Bureau of Justice Statistics, "National Sources of Law Enforcement Employment Data," US Department of Justice, 2016, https://bjs.ojp.gov/content/pub/pdf/nsleed.pdf.

and 23,272 EMS agencies.[3] Each of these agencies operates with its own set of policies, procedures, standards, and norms, which provides vast space for both gaps and overlap without some kind of organizing framework for coordination. In the UK, by contrast, there is a single organization that ostensibly manages all public safety agencies, which streamlines their ability to navigate and manage communication and increases their response speed. It's arguable that that system is more efficient than what we currently use in the United States.[4]

That's why school safety experts, including myself and my team at Joffe Emergency Services, have utilized the Incident Command System as a mechanism for managing school emergencies ranging from broad environmental disasters to isolated campus-based incidents. FEMA, the Federal Emergency Management Agency, has driven the adoption of the Incident Command System to be leveraged by all organizations responding to any emergency.

At Joffe, we use the FEMA model of ICS, and have adapted it to work in a school context. Others in the industry have done this as well, as FEMA's model is the Standard Incident Command Model (or the National Incident Management System, technically speaking), which is used for all emergencies across the country, ranging from car accidents to pandemics to major hurricanes. It's the same model that is used in the fire department, police departments, and municipality emergency management offices/ infrastructures. Because schools generally are smaller communities that have less infrastructure available to them than the large institutions that respond to national emergencies, we've adapted the model specifically to focus on the most critical roles and eliminate some of the layers of management that you might see in a military operation, for example.

---

[3]National Association of EMS Officials, "2020 NATIONAL EMERGENCY MEDICAL SERVICES ASSESSMENT," 2020, https://nasemso.org/wp-content/uploads/2020-National-EMS-Assessment_Reduced-File-Size.pdf.

[4]Laura H. Kahn and Jeremiah A. Barondess, "Preparing for Disaster: Response Matrices in the USA and UK," *Journal of Urban Health-Bulletin of the New York Academy of Medicine* 85, no. 6 (August 28, 2008): 910–22, https://doi.org/10.1007/s11524-008-9310-y.

Fundamentally, the Incident Command System is a composition of people, systems, resources, and processes that builds a chain of command, division of labor, and structure for decision making in emergencies. It's designed to ensure that information flows up the chain of command to a single person, known as the incident commander or the person in charge, and to ensure that decisions made at the top flow down through the chain of command to those involved in the response and recovery.

So what does the ICS system actually look like, and how does it work? Put in simple terms: ICS is an org chart for emergency response. The entire Incident Command System is designed around one single concept: to do the most good for the most people to ensure that in a situation where we have limited resources, the people who need those resources the most are receiving them.

We call the teams that respond to components of emergencies in the ICS model strike teams, which is a group of teachers and staff at a school who are assigned a certain set of tasks and then trained and prepared to do those tasks when an emergency hits. ICS is also designed to be flexible, so there are times when a school might decide to combine certain roles or teams (such as search and rescue and reunification), which is fine as long as it is done thoughtfully and all functions are covered by at least one or more roles. Additionally, as you build your teams, consider not only your primary team members but also who can take their place in the event that they aren't available when an emergency takes place. We generally recommend at least three to five but up to seven backups for each team.

Table 7.1 is a summary of the responsibilities for each role or strike team deployed using a typical school ICS model.

At Joffe, we use a few different models depending on charter vs. independent vs. public school and organizational design. Every structure will have at least the core (incident commander, strike teams, etc.), but you'll notice a few minor adjustments on these charts. For copies you can download and make your own, visit the accompanying website.

Table 7.1 Responsibilities for each role or strike team deployed using a typical school ICS model.

ICS Role/Team		Main Responsibilities
Incident commander		Oversees the full emergency response and activates internal strike teams. Fundamentally, this role is designed to process information and execute/communicate decisions.
Situation analysis team	Situation analysis leader	Responsible for the collection, organization, and analysis of incident status information and for analysis of the situation as it progresses. Keeps the incident commander informed of the incident. Oversees the documentation & timekeeping.
	Documentation & timekeeping	Overseen by situation analysis leader. Takes notes throughout an emergency or disaster including a running list of all events, the time of the events, participants, and significant impact throughout the incident.
Communications team	Communications team leader	Point of contact for incident command responsible for providing communication services throughout an incident to inform the school community of the situation. This may include drafting and sending phone calls /texts/emails as well as updating the school website and other social media; in some cases may involve media contact (contact your crisis communications partners for more detail there) and will always include building systems to listen, learn, and understand what's happening for the greater community. Oversees the public information officer & liaison.

(Continued)

ICS Role/Team		Main Responsibilities
	Public information officer & liaison	Overseen by communications team leader. The voice of the school in the event of an emergency. Communicates information to the press and/or news agencies. News media can play a key role in assisting the school with disseminating information related to emergencies or disasters to the public (parents). (Contact your crisis communications partners for more detail there.) Additionally, serves as the contact person for outside agencies: police, fire, ambulance services. May represent the school at city emergency operation centers and/or on-scene incident command.
■ Safety team	Safety director	Works to ensure that all activities are conducted in as safe a manner as possible under the existing circumstances. Establishes methods of communications with strike teams.
	Search & rescue	Locate and evacuate to safety any trapped, missing, or injured persons. Additional tasks are to identify dangers and provide safety during movements. Each sub-search team should be at least two people, ideally four.
	First aid & triage	Assess the extent of all injuries. Triage and tag the injured to be treated accordingly. Treat all injuries to the extent possible. See accompanying online guide for triage tags, guides, and tools.

ICS Role/Team		Main Responsibilities
	Crisis counseling	Works with first aid and community care to initiate response and monitor the well-being of individuals in psychological distress. (May be covered by the attendance team members.)
Community care team	Community care leader	Oversees all student and staff related needs.
	Attendance & assembly	Overseen by community care leader. The essential role at the onset of an emergency; knowing the overall status of all people on campus. This team needs to be aware of the entire campus community; those that serve on this team need to keep a wide outlook and be mindful of the typical people on campus as well as guests—substitute teachers, parent volunteers, outside vendors, or special guests.
	Reunification	Overseen by community care leader. Assures the reunification of students with their parents, authorized adults, or self-release at a predesignated area and makes sure students are properly signed out and accounted for before leaving campus.
Facilities & logistics:	Facilities and logistics	Responsible for shutting off gas, power, and water if needed. Will assess the stability and viability of buildings on campus to the best of their ability. Responsible for distributing and tracking supplies, mainly food and water, to students, faculty, and staff

(Continued)

ICS Role/Team	Main Responsibilities
	after an emergency. Will also assist with setting up shelter and toilet facilities if needed and with the distribution and transportation of strike team supplies as needed. Assures all work is done safely and in partnership with other teams. Oversees the work of site security.
Site security	Overseen by facilities & logistics leader. Acts to prevent any unintended, illegal, or unwarranted entries onto campus during the emergency. Directs fire, ambulances, and police to areas of need.

If you go back for a moment to the diagram on the prior page, you'll see that there are a set of teams in place that support this incident commander. Each of these teams has a critical role in navigating the emergency response and a specific set of responsibilities that they will respond to and that they will take charge of as the emergency response unfolds. This diagram offers a simple framework that I hope helps you put the practice of ICS into context. But, as in all things with emergency response, there are some complexities and nuances that are helpful to unpack. So let's do that.

> **Action Item:** Go to the website and download a copy of the org chart that matches your school type. Then, as you read through the descriptions, jot down names of the people on campus you'd want to assign to each role.

Incident Commander

In our school environments, the incident commander role is often assumed by the head of school, the superintendent, the principal, or the person who is typically in charge of the school (Figures 7.1

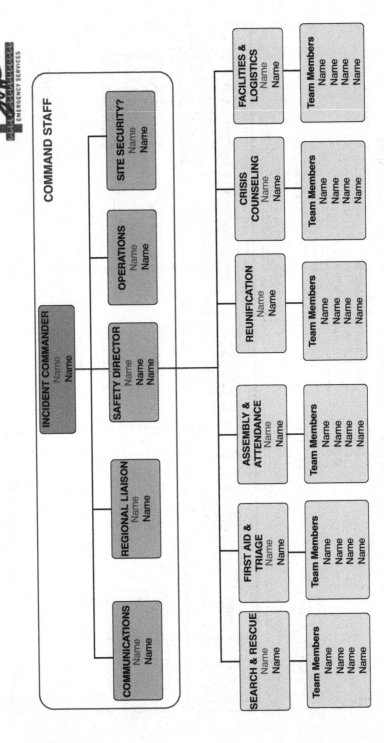

Figure 7.1: Joffe's incident command structure (1).

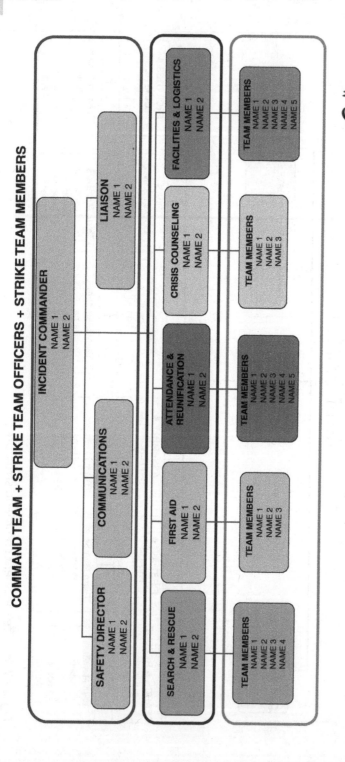

Figure 7.2: Joffe's incident command structure (2).

and 7.2). This is natural. The person who leads the school should be the person who leads the emergency response, right? Maybe. But maybe not.

Let's put that into context. Why did your head of school, your principal, or your executive director get hired to lead the organization day-to-day? Likely, it was because they have a set of leadership skills that help your school run more smoothly. Maybe they handle team building really well; or they're a strong educator or education leader; or they're a skilled fundraiser; or they know how to put out metaphorical fires when it comes to student- or family-related challenges, personnel, or legal issues.

Your leader *may* also happen to be good in a life-threatening emergency, and if that's the case, it makes perfect sense for them to be in the incident commander role. However, it's important for everyone (including the school leader themselves) to acknowledge that this ought not be a given. Responding to a crisis that has the potential to imminently threaten the health and safety of every member of your community is different from the skills that make a great educational leader, and sometimes these two skill sets are in different campus leaders.

The best person to lead in an emergency may be your director of operations, director of security, or director of fire and life safety. It may be any number of other folks. In fact, it could even be your science teacher, as we find every so often. **Consider the idea that the best person to lead the organization through the emergency may not be the head of school, principal, or executive director**.

We'll come back to the concept of incident commander. In this moment, I'd like to pivot and talk more about the teams of people that will support this leader, the teams of people that will guide the emergency response, and how information flows up and down through this system. For now, let's look at the structure of an ICS model.

Quick Tip on Incident Commanders

If you're a board member and you're going to interview a new head of school or you're a district leader who is going to hire a new principal and you want to ask them some related questions to understand their proclivity to get emergency management / incident command done well, here are a few questions you might consider asking:

1. When was the last time you were involved in a major emergency? What was your role? Was there a role you wish you played?
2. What are your priorities when responding to a major emergency?
3. What are your strategies for maintaining community values in parallel with managing a crisis?
4. How quickly should a school return after an emergency occurs? Why?
5. What are the biggest risks that come to mind in our school? Why?
6. Where is emergency preparedness and crisis readiness on your priorities list?
7. What role do you expect to play here in an emergency? And after an emergency?
8. How are you perceived in times of crisis, high stress, or in high-risk situations?

You're not looking for specific answers, per se, as much as engaging in a meaningful conversation about role, style, and strategy for managing emergencies.

Search and Rescue

Search and rescue has a central objective in the emergency response process. Their objective is to find, care for, recover, and relocate anybody who might be unaccounted for during an emergency. Put into context: If you are in California and there's a major earthquake; if you are in the Southeastern US and there's a major hurricane; if you are on a field trip in the wilderness, doing some sort of outdoor education program; and there's an issue where people are separated and somebody is missing, this is the team that jumps into action.

Search and rescue's job is often the job that takes place in the early part of the emergency response. It's the job that takes place while we wait for the fire department or other resources to arrive (or, in the event that we don't think they will arrive because of a major regional disaster, for example, this team acts in lieu of those agencies). In order to leverage time and start the response before the professionals get there, we want a group of essentially trained amateurs to take an initial pass.

Search and rescue is among the highest-risk roles, so it is particularly important for this team to be well trained and well prepared. Most importantly, they must know that their first priority must be their own safety. Under no circumstances should they put themselves in a position where they are not safe.

The team should be trained on the basics. They should be trained to have at least a searching crew of two or four so that if there were to be an aftershock or a subsequent emergency, there's somebody to help them. In EMS or the fire department, we call this the buddy system.

The team should be trained on the basics of what to look for in a building that they may or may not reenter. For example, if the building is a relatively new building, is at least apparently structurally sound, and there's a person who might be trapped, and we're expecting the fire department to be hours or even days away, we have to make a judgment call. Is it worth taking some risk for the person or persons on the search and rescue team to go into the building and try to find somebody who might be stuck, injured, or trapped? Or is it worth waiting and allowing the professionals to come and do it? We need to make sure that our search and rescue teams are empowered with the decision-making skills and that our incident commanders understand the risk associated with sending somebody into a building.

Furthermore, our search and rescue team members need to have some medical training so they can make smart decisions about moving people with injuries and also potentially treat those injuries while transporting them from point A to point B.

Finally, search and rescue team members should be trained on communication/collaboration because it is key. Identifying where people might be; collaborating with other teams to find out when the person was last seen; collaborating with other teams to determine what the potential risks are to the building; collaborating with external resources such as the fire department or building engineers to get input on whether it's reasonable to reenter the building, based on the set of circumstances that have been dealt. These things are all critical.

It's critical that the search and rescue team doesn't become injured or trapped themselves, so they should have ample training on strategies to keep themselves safe at all times.

Search and rescue can be used in a number of circumstances—following earthquakes, tornadoes, or building collapses, for example. One critical concept though is it should never be used if a building is on fire because we should never reenter a burning building under any circumstances. We should only allow the professionals to do so. Fire travels quickly. It often doubles in size every minute. Therefore, adding another person into that building without special gear and special training will more than likely put that person at risk and cause yet another person to need to be rescued, complicating the response for the fire department and increasing risk of additional injuries. More importantly, fires are generally "localized" emergencies. In the vast majority of fires, the fire department will be there very quickly, and therefore they can go in and rescue someone. This is directly in contrast to the earthquake scenario where the fire department might be three, or even more days away from being able to respond to your location for a rescue.

First Aid & Triage

What do we do when it comes to finding a person who's potentially injured and needs additional treatment? Enter the first-aid team. The first-aid and triage team has two essential functions: (1) first aid administers treatment to those who have physical injuries, and (2) using a system for triage, determines the severity of injuries and the priority level for treatment. Again, this team often acts while we wait for or, in worst-case scenarios, in lieu of responding agencies such as fire and EMS.

So who should be part of this team? In many schools, the first-aid team is led by the school nurse or health coordinator. This makes sense, as there's a natural connection there, and the leader of your health office will inevitably have the skills already to play this role. If your nurse or health coordinator works full time on your campus, having them lead the first-aid team is a sensible move. But for many schools, that's not the case. Just 34.5 percent of private schools have a full- or part-time school nurse, according to the National Association of School Nurses, which means that nearly two thirds of private schools do not have a full- or part-time nurse on campus.[5] For public schools, the number is much higher—81 percent—but I can tell you that many of the public schools we've worked with and spoken with over the years share their nurse with other schools across their district, which means they too may not have access to their nurse at the moment when an emergency strikes.

If your school is among the large proportion of schools that doesn't have a full-time medical provider on campus, you will need to consider who else can play the first aid and triage leadership role. Maybe it's an administrative assistant or a front desk administrator, an operations person, or a highly talented project or task manager who's familiar with the incident commander's leadership and communication style. If your nurse or health coordinator does happen to be on campus during a time when an emergency takes place, this will free them up to take on the role of primary health care provider, offering skilled treatment to the most challenging injuries rather than focusing on coordinating with other teams, as the first-aid team leader often must do. Of note, I actually prefer leaving an administrative person in charge of the team even if there *is* a full-time nurse / health care

---

[5]Willgerodt, M & Brock, D. (2016). NASN School Nurse Workforce Study. University of Washington.

practitioner on campus for the same reason. I'd rather have our health care folks doing health care vs. leading/managing the team (a highly task-oriented and administrative function).

In major emergencies, the first-aid team would also have the role of triage. To illustrate what triage means, I'll share a story one of my EMS instructors told me and my classmates during my first few weeks of training. He said:

> One day, you and your partner may be sitting at the station and get a call that a submarine or makeshift submarine was traveling up the coast from Mexico into Southern California, full of people who wanted to make their way into the country. And that boat or that submarine may capsize or take on water and present one of the worst-case scenarios that you can ever imagine.
>
> They may be spotted from the air. A call comes in to 911. You and your partner might be the first on scene, swim out to greet and meet this team of people or this community of people who need help, and be faced with 30, or 50, or 100 people who all need your help. In a worst-case scenario, none of these people may be able to swim, either because it took you so long to get there and they're beyond exhaustion or simply because they didn't have that skill set to begin with.
>
> And given the set of circumstances surrounding this transportation, it's unlikely that they will have buoyancy gear or anything else to help themselves. Put differently, it might be you that has swum out into the ocean, potentially in the middle of the night, and you might find 100 people who need your help. And you may have to make the choice with your partner which of those 100 people live and which will die.

I remember that distinctly, I think because at 17, that concept was absolutely terrifying to me. To this day, the thought of it still scares me. I was never put in that position, in quite that literal way, but throughout my career I have been confronted with this concept of choosing which people do and don't receive help. Even with training and expertise on the triage process, it can still be gut wrenching.

Fortunately, there's a system that can help those charged with triage make a thoughtful determination about who receives care. It's called START, and it was adopted by most responding agencies in the 1980s. It's designed to help the individual responder make the decision that most reliably and most consistently helps the people who are most savable and most in need of care.

Here is the basic premise:

Green represents the walking wounded. This is a term that says that the person has minimal injuries and that the person is going to be okay to sit and wait until they can be treated. For context, these are injuries such as a scrape, a scratch, a laceration that's bleeding but not severely, an injury to the body that, for all intents and purposes, is going to be okay.

One way to think about this is: If you walk into a room and say, "If you can hear me and you can stand, please stand up and walk outside," the people who follow your instructions and are able to walk outside would be considered green. This means they might have been stuck, injured, or affected at first, but were able to follow commands and self-evacuate to a position of safety.

The next category is yellow, the delayed category. Yellow includes people who have a serious but not life-threatening illness or injury. Ideally, this is assessed by the nurse or the health care provider who's on campus. However, it's important to note that often, this person will be busy treating people that are in the category above this and this assessment will need to be made by someone trained in triage.

To that end, additional folks on campus—science teachers, art teachers, specialists, PE teachers, others who can provide this basic level of first aid—should be trained on the START system too so that they can help with the intake process and with triaging people who need care and support. The premise around the walking wounded is that these people can wait, but not that long, for treatment. For example, a broken arm, a broken leg, or bleeding that is soaking through a few layers of gauze but not profuse or arterial in nature might put someone in the yellow category. At times, this can include head injuries or additional chronic injuries or illnesses as well.

Finally, the red category: immediate. These are the people who need to be treated right away; if they're not treated immediately, they will not survive. This category often includes people who have a gunshot wound, a femur break, a severe head injury, or most likely and most commonly during the events that we see in our schools, severe bleeding.

For this reason, those who are in the red category are often initially treated by search and rescue or someone else trained in first aid, and they're quickly shepherded to the first-aid and triage station for additional treatment. In the first-aid and triage station, they're first assessed and then treated and cared for. They are prioritized because if they are not treated now, they will die.

The last category, and the category that we struggle the most with in our school environments (and, frankly, the category that I even hesitate to include in this book) is known as the expectant or deceased category. This category includes those who have already passed or are not expected to survive.

Now, when we think about the category of people that fall into this group, we think about people who need CPR, or people who have had such severe bleeding that there's no way that they'll survive without additional blood being given—because in the field that's just not something that we have available.

We try to care for them with as much comfort and support as possible, but we recognize that we need to prioritize the people in the urgent (red) category, who have a greater chance of survival, before we prioritize these folks.

In short:

- BLACK (Deceased/expectant): injuries incompatible with life or without spontaneous respiration; should not be moved forward to the collection point;
- RED (Immediate): severe injuries but high potential for survival with treatment; taken to collection point first;

- YELLOW (Delayed): serious injuries but not immediately life-threatening;
- GREEN (Walking wounded): minor injuries.

There are emerging other systems that are out there; Jump-START, which considers the difference in "normal" respiratory rates for children, and SALT, which describes the overall process (sort, assessment, life-saving interventions, and treatment & transport) and gets treatment in play earlier in the process. The system adopted may be selected by your local office of emergency management already, so it's a good idea to check in with them before determining the triage and first-aid model you'll use.

One can upgrade and downgrade through these different categories—from green to yellow, or from yellow to red, or from red to black. They can also go the opposite direction. There are two levers that are pulled here: the first is the number of people who are being treated, and the second is the number of people who are available to treat.

Triage is, at its most fundamental level, a strategy to do the most good for the most people. If we have an unlimited number of responders and an unlimited number of people there who can provide help, then we can help every single person who needs it. This system becomes critical and it becomes the decision-making framework when we have a limited number of responders and a greater number of people who need help.

After Hurricane Ian came through in Florida in 2022, we saw this used. There were a limited number of people available to help, and it was unsafe for them to do so. Many of us watched on the news as firetrucks floated away from the fire department. Firefighters and paramedics worked simply to keep themselves safe while the hurricane passed through. In that instance, there were a limited number of responders and a huge number of people who needed help.

For that reason, anybody who could be treated was, but anybody who was either already gone or would have put rescuers in danger to try to treat was often considered not expected to survive.

This is a painful part of this work, but it's critical in service of triage. It's critical to do the most good for the most people.

Let's take this one step further. We have 10 people who are affected at an individual school campus, and we have five people who are trained in CPR, first aid, and maybe advanced first aid, who can provide support. Let's think for a moment about how those five people should be allocated. If we have five people that are in the red category—five people who are in the life-threatening illness or injury category—then each of those five people should likely be supporting, on a one-to-one basis, those in need. I realize that walking through this can be difficult and at times even scary. That's why we recommend building this framework into your trainings, and subsequently your drills, so everyone has an opportunity to understand it and try it before a real emergency occurs.

> **Action Item:** Conduct a drill where you test your first-aid team and give them a few different scenarios. Challenge them to determine which category folks might fall into. When we do drills in K–12 schools, we do not use the deceased category because it runs the risk of creating additional trauma in the preparedness process, and the goal is to build confidence, not fear.

If the idea of adding a triage process to your drills makes you nervous, you're not alone. But there are ways to help people practice triage without trauma. First, we recommend not including the black triage level in your drills, as it's generally highly sensitive and potentially triggering for people to think about how to respond to some who has lost their life. Stick with the green, yellow, and red categories, and get your team good at responding to those cases.

We do recommend convening a smaller group to discuss in a safe space (a small tabletop exercise or brainstorm session) what your approach would look like for anyone in the black category. Having this conversation will ensure the team has thought through your plan in advance. Keeping the audience limited will help your team stay engaged.

Crisis Counseling

What about the people who are not necessarily physically hurt but are psychologically injured? This is where we lean on the psychological first-aid (crisis counseling) team. Their job is to provide basic psychological care and to ensure that folks who need support are able to get it.

The psychological first-aid team should use the same concept—green, yellow, and red (no black)—to triage the people who need support. To begin with, everyone will start in the green category as everyone will need some sort of support following an emergency, but only a few will likely need immediate intervention. From there, you can prioritize the people who are already progressing into yellow or red.

This is particularly important to consider when somebody has a sibling, close friend, close teacher, parent, cousin, or any other close relationship with somebody else who's been injured. For example, if a student has a parent who also teaches at the school and the parent was injured during the emergency, we want to ensure that that student is placed in the red category right away—that that student is getting as close to one-on-one care as possible. We want to ensure that that student is also being isolated from the rest of the students in order to restrict the potential outburst that could affect other students and could progress other students into the yellow or red category.

The overall premise for psychological first aid and crisis counseling is: "Do everything you can to keep people as calm, collected, and as informed as possible." For people in the green category, you can do this by encouraging them to provide support for one another. Depending on the circumstances, this might involve having them sit in a field and just be together, talking to one another and (if possible) having a snack or meal together to process what they have just experienced together. Play games with students like capture the flag or kickball or monopoly to help them stay active, alert, and having fun, while creating a healthy distraction (if the circumstances are appropriate and safe to do so, of course). (**Pro tip**: Order boxes and boxes of pizza if this is an option to ensure people don't get too hungry, as this can exacerbate distress. They may not eat it right away, but having it as an option is always good.)

Our yellow category are folks that we're likely going to put into a group setting where they're working with either a counselor or a teacher who is proficient in mental health care—somebody who's been through trauma-informed practices training, somebody who has been through major emergencies even, perhaps, and learned from them some of the skills and mechanisms to help keep folks as calm, collected, and focused as possible.

Then, our red category are going to be people who are often one-on-one, or in some cases, even two-on-one—two adults with one student—being cared for as they navigate an acute psychological emergency.

Psychological first aid, at least for emergency response purposes, is a relatively new concept. Therefore, there's not as much infrastructure in place to manage it, but if you have a counselor on campus or you have access to a counselor, engaging them to help build your psychological first-aid team and psychological first-aid process is important.

At some schools, there's a student-led psychological first-aid team, which might look more like peer-to-peer support. In fact, peer-to-peer support is an excellent strategy for managing those in the green category and if necessary, can even be used to manage those in the yellow category.

These teams that I've talked about so far are teams that we hope not to use during emergencies. We hope that the emergency is fast enough, or rather the response from our supporting agencies is fast enough, that we don't need to activate them. If we do need to activate them, these teams—search and rescue, first aid, and psychological first aid—are going to need an abundance of support along the way, as well as care after the emergency is complete.

They will make hard decisions—decisions that could have impacts on others—and they will need to understand this in advance. They should also be protected and supported after the fact, with a reassurance of their safety, counseling, and (in the most challenging circumstances) physical security to keep them from becoming the target of others' anger or grief. These teams are our embedded heroes. These are the teams that you should go out and build today so that when an emergency happens, no matter how isolated or how significant, your school has the independence it needs to be able to operate while you wait for new resources to arrive.

The next set of teams will activate in every emergency. They are no less critical. But they are teams that will get to practice and engage on a very frequent basis.

Attendance and Assembly

I choose to start with the attendance and assembly team because it's a place where schools can build from existing processes and strengths. Why? Because most schools do attendance at least once a day, so they have infrastructure and processes to lean on. But, unsurprisingly, there are some nuances and differences between taking attendance during the regular school and taking attendance during an emergency.

Many schools will take attendance at the beginning of each class or at the beginning of each homeroom. Nonetheless, teachers have practiced taking attendance. As it turns out, just like anything else in an emergency, attendance after the emergency has occurred is slightly different and therefore requires a different area of focus, a different team dynamic, and a few nuances.

When we take attendance during the day on a regular day, we are able to walk through a list in our online system and say, "Is so and so here? Is so and so here?" As we do that, we're using technology. We're using power. We're using Wi-Fi or cell service. We're using light in the classroom. Truth be told, when we talk about emergency attendance, we need to design a program and a system that doesn't rely on any of those things.

One of the most common mistakes our schools make when it comes to attendance is simply printing out the attendance logs for every single period and having those available in the teacher's backpack, and having those available outside, wherever students, faculty, and staff might congregate after the emergency occurs. The problem with this strategy is that attendance lists change! In many cases, they change weekly, even. Students add/drop classes, move between schedules, and that leaves a teacher (especially a substitute) vulnerable to missing a student who might've been newly added or searching for a student who may have been dropped from their class.

The second, and arguably more challenging, piece to consider is taking attendance for adults. Most schools don't have a mechanism in place for this and aren't regularly taking this on. We might know on any given day which teachers did not come to school because we needed to get subs for their classes, but what about the ones who might have left campus during a break, or popped over to the district office for something? On a regular day this doesn't necessarily matter, but when an emergency takes place, not knowing who is on or off campus at that moment becomes a problem because we don't know who is missing and needs to be found. If you don't already have one in place, it's important to figure out a mechanism to take attendance for adults on campus. To track staff and faculty, some schools use a whiteboard by the door, and faculty and staff will simply write their name on the board as they leave and erase their name from the board as they arrive.

Others choose to do it through badge systems. Again, if you're using a badge system, like an access control reader, that's okay if you have a continuous print of who's on-campus and off-campus, which does waste paper but ensures that, if power, Internet, or other services go down, you have access. It's not perfect, and it can be redundant if there's a paper backup being created in real time.

But what about visitors and vendors? A parent reading in a second-grade classroom, a plumber fixing a pipe, a reading specialist working with a student. These all need to be accounted for.

Most schools are better at tracking vendors and visitors than faculty and staff, largely because visitors and vendors are typically transient. Therefore, most schools have them check in using a visitor management system when they arrive, and some also have them check out when they leave (an important practice to implement if you don't do this already, since it helps ensure you know when visitors are no longer on campus).

We can get into the details of a visitor management system in dialogue, but the core competencies of any visitor management system, or VMS, are that they are capable of tracking people who arrive on campus. Ideally, they're capable of conducting a sex offender screening, because this is an important best practice and ensures your system is set up in the event that this is or becomes a requirement.

The visitor management system should also feed into a continuous printer of some sort or should be mimicked by a paper process to ensure that, if power, Internet, or other infrastructure go down, we still have access to those logs. Our attendance process should follow, roughly, this outline. The bell should go off, and everyone evacuates. Staff, faculty, and leadership assemble students in the primary, secondary, or tertiary assembly locations. Attendance then walks through and makes sure that all students are accounted for, while a second team, faculty and staff attendance, reconciles the list for all faculty and staff. A third sub-team on the assembly and attendance team accounts for visitors, vendors, parents, and others who might be on campus.

In walking through this process, we should aim to complete the attendance in two to four minutes. Depending on the size of your school, you may be able to get it done more quickly, but this is the goal. After the initial attendance process is complete, we should plan to retake attendance every hour or so to ensure no one has gone missing since we started.

In the hospital, for example, if you are in for a critical incident, they will take your vital signs when you first arrive, and then they'll retake those vital signs every few minutes in order to make sure that they're staying on top of changes and tracking trends. If you're a stable patient, it may be an hour—sometimes even longer—before they reassess those vital signs.

Attendance should follow a similar process. Once the group is stable, in a safe (ideally enclosed) location, attendance should be taken approximately every hour.

If there is any instability (parents or police arriving and departing, open space where students can easily wander off, or other vulnerable conditions), we should be reassessing attendance every 15 or 30 minutes. Our goal is to ensure that if somebody is missing, we identify who and notify search and rescue, to activate their process as quickly as possible. The faster we begin to look for someone, the more concrete information we will have about where they were last seen, and the closer they will typically be to the place where they were last seen (read: the more likely they are to be found).

Once attendance is stable, we shift into assembly, where students and staff stay together in a safe, predesignated location to wait for the emergency response process to play out.

Access to bathroom facilities, food, water, and some sort of activity are important here. The assembly team are also adjuncts to the physical and psychological first-aid team, keeping eyes and ears out for a student or staff member who might be in distress and notifying those support teams for intervention as needed.

Reunification

The next step is the reunification process. If attendance is most practiced, reunification is probably the least practiced of all of the teams in this section. Let's start by defining reunification. In its simplest form, reunification is the process of reuniting students with their parents or guardians at the end of the emergency. It's essentially an emergency version of dismissal.

If that idea makes you nervous, you're in good company. When I ask leaders of schools or members of school communities to tell me about dismissal, they typically get uneasy. Because, if we're being honest, dismissal is a challenge for many, many schools.

But there's some good news about reunification that will be an asset in your emergency dismissal process. The first is that at this stage of the emergency, you will have much of your staff and faculty back from their original strike team duties because now, search and rescue is complete, attendance is done, and triage is likely complete. Now, it's time for everyone on campus to focus on how to get students back to their families safely, and you will have more staff and faculty available to play a role in that process. We'll circle back to more detail around reunification once we orient you to the elapsed time that we experience during emergency response.

Team Leadership

As you consider how to build each team, it's important to consider the role of the team leader. It may sound counterintuitive, but the best people to be team leaders are not necessarily tactical people with expertise in that area but people who are good managers and delegators. Why? Because in crisis moments team leaders will be responsible for ensuring people are where they need to be, that they have what they need to be successful, and that other teams are clearly informed of progress and obstacles.

Said differently, for our psychological first-aid team, if we have our school counselor or social worker as the team leader, they will not be positioned well to actually provide care (the role they're most trained for). We want them to be providing a ton of psychological first aid during those moments, not coordinating and communicating with other teams. We'd be better served for our front desk manager, or our business office manager, or another person to take the role and responsibility of communicating with the command team and relaying that information down to the rest of the team.

Either way, one of the keys to success in ICS team building is redundancy. That's a fancy way of saying backups, essentially ensuring you have multiple people in a line of succession to play the role of each team leader and team member if needed. Again, we recommend having at least three, ideally five to seven backups for each role to ensure your school is well covered and can play each vital function. Because no matter how prepared we are, if we are operating without teammates to play some of our key roles, it will be hard to have a successful response.

"First On" Leadership

In the National Incident Management System (NIMS) language, there's a concept called "First On" that is valuable to know about for school emergencies. Essentially, the concept is that the first person to arrive at the emergency is the incident commander until somebody else of equal or greater training takes over. So if you are a teacher in a classroom and a student is having a seizure and you're the only teacher in that classroom, you're the incident commander. When a school nurse comes in, that person then takes over as the incident commander. If you're a security officer and you discover a suspicious package, you're the incident commander until the police arrive to investigate.

We have an entire segment of this book dedicated to leadership and communication, which are truly the foundation of successful emergency response, but know this: The greatest responsibility of an incident commander is to be the leader and to communicate and receive communication. So if you happen to be the first person to show up or become aware of an emergency, it's up to you to take responsibility for that emergency, to take leadership, and to start communication because if not you, then who?

While this chapter is relatively thorough there's certainly much more to learn and explore when it comes to ICS. I chose to focus on a few roles and teams specifically here because they are highly nuanced. But there are some I have not explained in detail here, and for those, you can review the accompanying web page for this book, which offers a variety of additional resources and best practices. Most successful schools invest in safety and security as a full community and a rough structure to help you plan your year. It's critical to double-check your local laws and regulations and be compliant first with those, but in general, Table 7.2 gives you an idea of total time invested by the most successful schools I work with.

Table 7.2 Annual schedule template for crisis response training.

What?	When?	How Much?	Details
Faculty/staff orientation to safety	Intro-week	60–90 minutes	Default responses (what do we do in the event of our top risks)
Faculty/ staff CPR/ first aid/AED training	Intro-week *Many schools alternate year over year, which cuts time in half	~7 hours	Include Epi-Pens, Bleeding Management, asthmatics, student action plans
Faculty/staff tabletop	Intro-week	75 minutes	Pick your highest-risk item and talk through with all teams
Faculty/staff strike team trainings	Before start of school	60 minutes didactic 60 minutes practical	Just those adults who have been assigned to a strike team to serve
Drill	August	30 minutes	Include debrief; always clarify that it's a drill at the start
Drill	September	30 minutes	Include debrief; always clarify that it's a drill at the start
Drill	October	30 minutes	Include debrief; always clarify that it's a drill at the start
Drill	November	30 minutes	Include debrief; always clarify that it's a drill at the start

(Continued)

What?	When?	How Much?	Details
Drill	December	30 minutes	Include debrief; always clarify that it's a drill at the start
Faculty/staff training for larger drill (if planned)	January	45 minutes	Retouch training from fall, prepare for reunification drill
Drill	January	30 minutes	Include debrief; always clarify that it's a drill at the start
Drill	February	30 minutes	Include debrief; always clarify that it's a drill at the start
Drill	March	30 minutes	Include debrief, always clarify that it's a drill at the start
Drill	April	60–90 minutes	Conduct reunification drill
Drill	May	30 minutes	Include debrief; always clarify that it's a drill at the start
Drill	June	30 minutes	Include debrief; always clarify that it's a drill at the start
		~14 hours (If you do CPR/first-aid training on alternate years)	

The numbers might surprise you, and you might be anxious around the concept of investing 14 hours every year into safety efforts. The reality is that it may not be achievable every year, but it is achievable as you're developing a culture around safety, and it's very achievable, especially in the years where you plan to conduct a reunification drill. I'd argue that it should occur no less than every other year to train not only teachers but also parents, and even students. If your drills are seven minutes right now, try bumping them to 12 first; don't go straight to 30, but start working on making them more meaningful by pulling a student out of line or taking some of the other actions we've defined throughout this book.

The reality is that each of these teams can and should be preestablished, pretrained, and fully functional before the emergency starts. If you find yourself in a new school, working with new colleagues, or otherwise not fully trained when you face an emergency, the most important action a leader (of any level) can take is to establish leadership and begin communicating. If you do that, at the very least, you've established some time for external rescuers to arrive and help support the ongoing emergency response.

III

The Seven Circles: A Framework for Emergency Response and Recovery

In this part, we'll explore a few different emergencies from the lens of time. We'll discuss the beginning, middle, and end, but we'll explore this through a series of "7s," which we use to teach the evolution of crisis. Sometimes the most debilitating part of a crisis is simply not knowing what is coming next. To that end, I believe that sharing what you can expect—along with what you can do—at different stages of an emergency is inherently empowering and enables you to plan for and work through the evolution of a given crisis. We'll also reflect here on how the concentric circles that we've just learned about can be put into action differently at different phases of the emergency.

I created the rule of 7s to simply help people wrap their minds around the evolving priorities at different times of the emergency.

I'm often asked why seven, and there are a few pieces of elegance that I'll share with you throughout Part III, but importantly, if you prefer 3s, 5s, or 9s, you could use those, too, I suppose. But stick with 7s for at least the remainder of this book, and I hope you'll find there's some real power in the framework.

7 seconds
7 minutes
7 hours
7 days
7 weeks
7 months
7 years

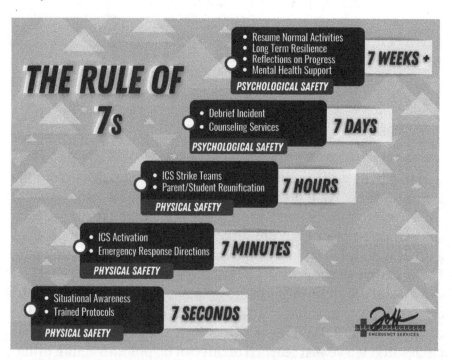

8

Initiation
The First
Seven Seconds

Focus: Determining it's an emergency, deciding to act, establishing leadership to solicit support.

In the first seven seconds of an emergency, our most central focus (which, as we'll find, is the foundation for the entirety of the emergency) is about ensuring that first we and then those around us are physically safe. Ideally, we'll also do some communication and leadership (yelling, "Lockdown" or hitting a panic button, etc.), but we should only do those things if we are, first ourselves, physically safe. This must be our initial priority and an underlying goal throughout the entire crisis response.

Think about a major emergency that you've heard of or maybe even experienced. A fire, a flood, an earthquake, a car accident. We've already addressed the reality that you may have a period of denial. Take a moment, now, and count out loud: one thousand one, one thousand two, one thousand three, one thousand four, one thousand five, one thousand six, one thousand seven. That's seven seconds. From that exercise alone, we can detect how quickly this moves and how important it is that we make some decisions—including the decision to act—today, proactively, so that when we're faced with the emergency, we simply leverage our well-established neural pathways we discussed previously in order to activate the appropriate response for the given situation.

The painful reality is that the first seven seconds are largely going to come down to your training, your muscle memory, your physical/psychological state (fatigue, intoxicants, etc.), and your capacity for overcoming denial.

I'll use small planes as one example, here. I fly a small, single-engine plane. It goes up as high as about 14,000 feet, but obviously in order to take off and land, I spend a lot of time close to the ground. When I take off, one of the emergencies I was trained for was that my engine could die upon leaving the runway (when you take off in a small plane, you push the gas as far forward as you can—like flooring it in a car). Doing so is typically the first time you've set the power that high since the engine was started, and therefore, any number of potential risks could play out. Of course, you do tests on the ground, check as you add power, and so forth, but at the end of the day, there's still a risk the engine could cut out. When you leave the runway, the nose of the airplane is pointed up (just like when you take a commercial flight).

In this scenario, if you lose your engine at 500–1,000 feet, you quite literally have seconds before you become a paperweight falling out of the sky. How many seconds? Probably less than 10 depending on a variety of factors if you're at 500 feet. Can you recover after that? Maybe if you're talented. But let's be clear, if you're really talented, you've trained for those first few seconds so much that your body takes over and you automatically do the things you need to, including some which might feel counterproductive to keep you, your passengers, the airplane, and the people on the ground safe. Can you talk to air traffic control for help? Honestly, no. You can't expect yourself to be able to convey the problem and receive a response that you can then interpret and execute within 7–10 seconds. It's just not realistic. Your training, your copilot if you have one, and your available safety features in your plane (parachute or whatever) are all you have. Therefore, you train from your earliest flights forward for this scenario.

Now, let's take this back into a school-based emergency but see if we can capture the same tenets. In a school, perhaps the most devastating community-wide emergency that nearly all of us would include on our risk assessment is an active shooter. In an active shooter event, we have seconds to default to progress and then execute on that progress (obviously depending on where they are relative to us in the building).

Here again, the truth is that there is very little chance that you're going to get a notification or confirmation of what's happening immediately. We want to accelerate the notification process as much as humanly possible such that more people are notified more quickly. That said, if you're near the location of the shooter, it's highly unlikely that you'll receive any useful directions before it's too late to act. You're left with your ability to recognize the sounds or signs and then default to progress.

How do we make the most of the first seven seconds?

We take distinct action today. We've talked throughout the book about the importance of training, of practice, of empowerment of individual teachers, staff, and maybe even students. If you're an on-campus school leader (a head of school, a principal, or similar), teaching your team to act **independent of you** in these first few moments is critical. What should that training look like?

In your risk assessment, you uncovered a series of potential high-risk (high severity, high likelihood) events. Take a moment to reflect on those, and hopefully your list has two to six items in the time-critical safety area. For the purposes of this explanation, I'll use an earthquake because whether you're in earthquake territory or not, you can likely imagine the massive impact of that—and it's slightly less frightening than a discussion about active shooters.

Your goal in training is to ensure that your teachers and staff will take the right actions for physical safety from the moment the earthquake starts to the moment the earthquake ends. It's safe to assume that the most damaging earthquakes will go on more than seven seconds (on average earthquakes run from about 10–30 seconds).[1] You are not going to be in every place at the same time on campus.

The earth starts shaking. Right now. What are you supposed to do? What keeps you safe?

This isn't a test. Here's what you do:

1. Drop, cover, hold! If you're in earthquake territory now or if you grew up in earthquake territory, you recognize these words. You're supposed to drop to the ground, take cover under a table, chair, or something sturdy, and then hold on.

I realize that during drills, you're likely the one "creating the earthquake" by getting on your PA system, or perhaps even shouting down the hallways or something along those lines, so in practice, you actually have not been doing a lot of "Drop, cover,

---

[1]University of Utah, "Frequently Asked Earthquake Questions," U Of U Seismograph Stations, 2023, https://quake.utah.edu/earthquake-information-products/earthquake-faq.

hold"–type work. But again, this is a real emergency, so your job is to first get yourself into a position of physical safety and second bring folks you can see, reach, or communicate to in the process along with you.

While you're under the desk, table, or chair, could you yell to others to drop, cover, and hold? Sure! But are you going to be able to yell over all that's going on in the gym across campus? No. Those folks—at the very least the adults—need to have the skills to drop, cover, and hold on their own and to do the same with the students around them.

At this point, I hope we can agree on this. If you don't agree with me, if you still think you can direct people's action during the first seven seconds of an earthquake, then give me a call because I may have a job for you at a safety training company!

We've got to ensure that we get everyone on campus ready to respond to those first seven seconds in a consistent way. Here's the template:

We want everyone to:

1. Get into a position of physical safety for themselves and those around them;
2. Begin to contemplate psychological safety as practical (in this case, there's not much we can do, yet);
3. Communicate;
4. Establish or fall in line with leadership.

What if it's an active shooter or a tornado? Same guideposts. What if it's a wildfire? Same guideposts. The first seven seconds play out using these initiatives as scaffolding, regardless of the emergency. How we do that can be debated; below we'll address a few of the competing philosophies for managing the first seven seconds of different types of emergencies, but in general, we're working to first get into a position of physical safety, and if we don't have time to do anything more, that's okay, in these first seven seconds, but we would continue down the list (almost like a checklist) if we had the time.

At this point, let's think about the *how*, which is so complex in a school environment that if you're not deeply invested in the *why*, you won't succeed at planning out the *how*. There are simply too many competing demands for time, resources, and focus, and you've got to enter from a place of clarity, or you won't get the time and energy you need.

How do we influence the first seven seconds of a crisis? It starts today.

Confucius said, "I see and I forget. I hear and I remember. I do and I understand."

I am not, myself, an educator. If you are, you likely know more about the learning process and pathway to stickiness than I do. If you're an educator, I challenge you to use the same pedagogical philosophy you use with your students when it comes to teaching your community how to manage crises, with a few general guidelines that I'll offer to help you stay focused and ensure it translates to emergency situations, too (Figure 8.1). If you're not an educator, this is a great place to bring in your academic team to explore!

Teaching: A few times per year, there should be conversations about safety and security on campus. Ideally, your safety leader leads these sessions. That helps reestablish their credibility and leadership in this area and is highly practical because they're the ones who are most engaged in the day-to-day crises (the small stuff) that comes up on every campus. They can tie in lessons from the smaller events in order to help the entire community scaffold up to the larger events. In the most successful schools I've seen,

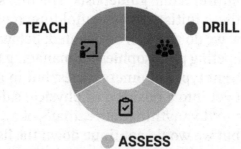

Figure 8.1: Drill Cycle

these make up about two hours of time per year. Often, there's a 90-minute session in the beginning of the school year (July or August typically before students come back for a nine-month school calendar) and then a follow-up discussion in January as a midyear touchpoint.

These trainings should include the items that came up in red and yellow on your risk assessment. In general, there are two ways that people train on emergencies. Input-based or output-based. At Joffe Emergency Services, we've tried both. I Love U Guys Foundation, a nonprofit group that has developed a model called the Standard Response Protocol, has also chosen a response-based protocol.[2] Interestingly, I often find that if you have a local firefighter or police officer lead training, they'll choose input-based. This isn't wrong, per se, but the training can be dense and often leaves people with more choices to make. Furthermore, it's the way that police officers and firefighters are trained, so it makes sense that they'd translate that same approach to educators. The difference is, they're also trained substantially on how to default to progress, so they're more likely to be successful in navigating the sea of choices available to them to make specific definitions.

Input-based training: In the event of a falling aircraft, you should do X; in the event of a fire, you should do Y.

Output-based training: A falling aircraft would create a fire and/or explosion. In general, we want to move away from that. So use the evacuation response. Incidentally, if you're in/on the falling aircraft, that's a different issue and one you don't have much control over. Unless, you're flying the falling aircraft, but I digress.

Approximate time allocation: two hours.

The first seven seconds is about influencing the behaviors, psychology, and actions that people take before the event occurs. It's about practicing and imparting strength to teachers who will become leaders in the initial moments of the emergency,

[2]SRP. The "I Love U Guys" Foundation, n.d., https://iloveuguys.org/The-Standard-Response-Protocol.html.

Table 8.1 Key lessons, steps, and roles.

Key lesson:	The first seconds of an emergency are managed before the emergency ever happens.
Key step:	Physical safety
Key roles:	
Teachers/staff:	Default to progress
Leaders:	Default to progress
Students:	Follow directions
Parents:	Likely don't even know about the emergency yet
Board:	Likely don't even know about the emergency yet

and it's about ensuring that every single person has a "default response" to take in response to different surrounding concerns (Table 8.1). Most importantly, in the first seven seconds, everyone is the incident commander of their own space; we're using the "First on" concept until we can replace it with something better. So make sure everyone knows how to take the first actions with independence. In our next chapter, we walk through what happens in the first seven minutes.

> **Action item:** Prepare faculty/staff to take the correct actions in the first seven seconds. This probably looks like a combination of training and practice.

9

Activation
The First
Seven Minutes

- Establishing physical safety;
- Initial steps for psychological safety;
- Calling for emergency response;
- Initiating ICS;
- Potentially, communication to families.

One of my favorite principals I've ever spoken with is named Linda Cliatt-Wayman. Principal Wayman delivered a TED Talk in 2015. In her talk, she teaches some of her philosophies on developing strong schools, engaging students, and leadership. One of the mantras she uses is simple yet powerful: "If you're gonna lead, lead." The first seven minutes are the first opportunity you have as a school leader to lead your school through crisis. Laying the groundwork for this specific response began long before the event. You had to get buy-in for the safety program so that you could influence the first seven seconds and your leadership will persist beyond the event. We'll talk about for how long, but these seven minutes are your first moment after the emergency has begun to establish and maintain leadership.

How We Make the Most of the First Seven Minutes

Much like the first seven seconds, most of the first seven minutes are prescribed well before the emergency happens. But there are some differences in what you need to have done beforehand. First, let's talk about the core principles, and then we can get into the tactics.

We want everyone to:

1. Get into a position of physical safety for themselves and those around them;
2. Begin to contemplate psychological safety as practical;
   a. Note: Here, you might be able to start to talk with students, engage about what happened and what you're

doing to keep them safe, etc. Situation dependent, but we can take an active role in psychological safety through dialogue and what they are (or more likely aren't) exposed to;

3. Communicate;
4. Establish or fall in line with leadership.

If those look familiar, then you're paying attention. Great!

Physical safety in the case of a student having a seizure is much more about that student themselves. We want to start first aid and ensure that we dial 911 as appropriate, leveraging our school health resources, and so forth. There's limited, if any, danger being created by this situation for other students. But, here, for the first time, we have the time to think about psychological safety. I've learned of a few circumstances where a student was experiencing a seizure and other students pulled out their phones and videoed the seizure. There was probably no mal intent, but we've seen that turn into a bullying situation. During a seizure, often people lose control of their bowels, they may vomit, or become incontinent, which can be especially difficult to recover from socially if you're a middle schooler or high schooler. Seeing the images on social media could make it impossible to ever feel psychologically safe in that school or community again. So tactics such as having students clear the room, having the security leader who responded to the room take over patient care *or* taking the other students across the hall to another teacher's room are strategies that we can use to create psychological safety for all students.

In this case, our communication could have been automated if we had our VOIP (Voice Over Internet Phones—which is a fancy way of saying your phones were purchased after ~2015 and are connected through the Internet instead of through a plain old telephone service) systems or had walkie-talkie radios—both great tools to empower people in the community to respond. In both cases, 911 protocols can be established notifying administrators of the 911 call in order to cause more help to arrive at the classroom.

Why Seven Minutes?

People often ask me why we use seven minutes as the next threshold. In part, it's that the rule of 7s sounds nice. But there's a more jarring reason, too. In the United States, the National Fire Protection Association, NFPA, creates standards under which fire departments are expected to operate. One of those standards, NFPA Standard 1710, details the time that a responding agency can take to get to a call. If you live in a major urban area, there's a good chance that your fire department is rated as a Class 1 Response Agency. This generally means that they're fast to respond to calls and do so with the right resources a majority of the time. Let's take a moment to walk through what happens, though, not on campus, but regarding your critical helpers, the fire department, EMS, and other agencies who are going to respond. This will help establish the *why* behind our independence for the first few minutes of an emergency.

- **Emergency:** Let's use the previously mentioned medical emergency: a student has a seizure in class.
- **Catalyst (0 seconds):** Student begins seizing.
- **Denial (3–10 seconds):** That's not really happening. (Note: If 10 seconds feels like an excruciatingly long amount of time to be in denial, it is. But in my experience, it's common enough to contemplate).
- **Call (90 seconds):** The teacher calls 911 and speaks to a dispatcher:
  - "911 emergency. What is your emergency?"—dispatcher begins processing the call discussing with the teacher what's going on and what resources are needed.
  - Dispatcher now begins multitasking. (Note: Dispatchers are among the most unsung heroes of any emergency response.)
    - Dispatcher is sending a local resource (fire truck, ambulance, police officer, whatever resources are appropriate) to the school.

- Simultaneously, the dispatcher is beginning to walk the teacher through what to do to help make the situation better.
- **Pro Tip:** It's valuable, if you have VOIP phones, to have your phones automatically notify a small group of people on campus about a 911 call. Using that, they can start to head toward the classroom where the call was placed to begin to provide support. If you do have this resource, the small group of people should generally include:
  - On-campus health contact (nurse, health coordinator, EMT, etc.);
  - On-campus security contact;
  - Office manager/receptionist;
  - The health and security contacts should respond to the room and then your office manager/receptionist can notify the principal/head of school and begin to coordinate for the arrival of EMS/police, etc.

To get to this point, it's taken about 90 seconds. I'll give you the times as we continue forward.

- **Turnout time (80 seconds):** The local resources are engaged at this point, so the firefighters, paramedics, and others drop everything and get to their vehicles. The turnout time is the time it's allowed to take for those resources to get into their gear and get to their vehicles. This is approximately 80 seconds.[1] It's important to note that they're trying to be faster than that, but sometimes our helpers are in the middle of a shower, a restroom break, cooking a meal, etc., and all those things need to come to a safe halt before they can come and respond to an emergency.

---

[1]"FIRE RESPONSE TIME," Fems, n.d., https://fems.dc.gov/page/fire-response-time.

- **Getting there (4 minutes):** Then, the vehicle(s) drive to your location. Often, we assume that lights and sirens mean they'll be there immediately, but the reality is that takes time, too. In 2021, the NFPA captured about 36.5 million calls that the fire departments alone ran in the United States.[2] It's critical that each of those calls be run with careful regard for not just the patient they're coming to serve but also the public that stands between them and the patient. I've driven on these responses and at times had cars on the road dart out in front, try to pass, motion that my siren was too loud for them to continue their phone call (while driving). Ninety percent of the time, this is expected to be less than 240 seconds, so approximately 4 minutes go by at this phase.
- **Contact (30–60 seconds):** Then, they arrive to help, at which point they're going to need to find the patient(s) in need of care. This takes another 30 seconds or more. (**Pro Tip:** Have someone meet the responding agencies out front if it's practical and safe to do so. You know your access points, classroom numbers, and locations best. The ideal situation is that your security leader radios your receptionist to a specific room and strategy for helping EMS get onto campus (in this scenario), and then the receptionist can greet the responding agency and walk them straight to the space where they're needed.)

All in, this is about 420 seconds (seven minutes) from the time that the initial emergency occurred. Of course, there is care and support happening along the way, the dispatcher is providing guidance, the teacher is providing first aid, but it takes time before help arrives. Therefore, you need to be a leader in the first seven minutes. Those minutes are going to provide a foundation for how the rest of the emergency will progress and how the emergency

---

[2] "NFPA Statistics—Fire Department Calls," n.d., https://www.nfpa.org/News-and-Research/Data-research-and-tools/Emergency-Responders/Fire-department-calls.

Table 9.1 What happens when you call 911.[3]

Step/phase	What's happening?	Time taken (seconds)	Elapsed time from start (seconds)
Catalyst	Student begins seizing	0*	0
Denial	That's not really happening	10*	10
Default to progress	The teacher calls 911. . . teacher is on hold	15	25
911 engages	911 operator picks up: "911. What is your emergency?"	64	89
Dispatched resource	911 operator guides teacher on what to do while dispatching local resources Teacher might begin to move other students out of the room	68*	
Turnout	Local resources get to their vehicle	60	149
Drive time	Local resources drive from station to scene	240	389
On scene locating	Local resources arrive on scene, looking for patient/classroom	30+	419

*Anecdotal, not sourced from the same data set

---

[3]Data taken from the source "NFPA 1710: Standard for the Organization and Deployment of Fire Suppression Operations, Emergency Medical Operations, and Special Operations to the Public by Career Fire Departments," n.d., https://www.nfpa.org/codes-and-standards/all-codes-and-standards/list-of-codes-and-standards/detail?code=1710.

will be remembered. Was it traumatic? Was it organized? Did we communicate effectively? Can we be trusted to run future emergencies? Fair or not, these are just a few of the questions that teachers and staff will ask and students will discuss.

I've provided two useful references that summarize the above scenario (Table 9.1, Figure 9.1). Often, we can become frustrated with how long it takes for our 911 resources to arrive. However, if you understand what is going on along the way, you can empathize and know that they are getting there as quickly as possible, and you can take greater responsibility for the first few minutes.

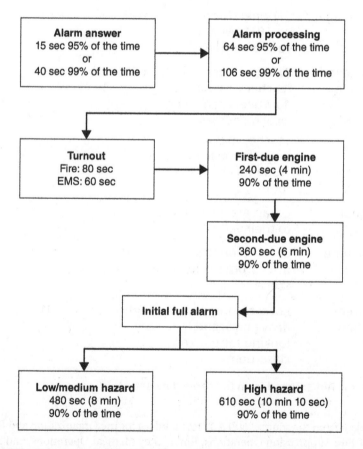

Figure 9.1: Response objectives from the National Fire Protection Association.[4]

---

[4]Data taken from the source "List of NFPA Codes and Standards."

These times are reliable 90 percent of the time. However, there is an aging population, and our public service careers have larger labor shortages than ever before. Given this, it's likely that these times will grow, not shrink over time. Furthermore, the volume of calls has been rising on average 3 percent per year over the last 41 years (1980–2021). There are *fewer* people responding to *more* calls in *more* congested cities. I argue that for those reasons, an increasing responsibility exists for schools to engage the right people on campus to both mitigate the need for 911 calls and ensure that when we do need 911, we're using the resource effectively. For example, have a health-care professional on campus so that you can treat the things that can be treated on campus instead of leveraging the 911 system and when that professional needs help and dials 911, have someone meet 911 at the street, be quick, have paperwork ready if the student needs transportation to the hospital, etc. (**Pro Tip:** There are electronic health record systems out there like Magnus Health that enable you to print a 911 card so that you can simply hand that to the paramedics and they can in turn hand it to the hospital staff. By providing a tool like that, the student can be treated appropriately [the right medications, history, and allergies are known] and the paramedics don't have to spend time writing up a history from the nurse's memory.)

The counter to everything I've just laid out is that there are truly extenuating circumstances on either side of this equation:

Delayed response: Earthquake, tornado, etc. It shouldn't be a surprise that in cases where an entire geographic community is affected, the responding agencies will take substantially longer to respond. In California, for example, we talk about three to seven days of independence (that's a nice way of putting it) after a major earthquake occurs. For that reason, schools should equip themselves with even more resources to ensure they can endure that period of independence. We talk more about this in Chapter 11.

Accelerated response: Active shooter. It shouldn't be a surprise that in cases where a single location—school or otherwise—has an active shooter, a response will be substantially faster than in other cases. Quite literally, the police officer on a traffic stop will leave the traffic stop, the county sheriff will dispatch nearly all their resources, the mutual aid programs (a partnership that all public agencies have where they rely on one another for support in critical times) will activate, and what feels like every resource in the world will descend on the school very quickly. It still won't be immediate, but it will be quick.

Critical context: Most active shooter events are over in minutes. We've seen a few outliers, but as an average, the violence has concluded by this point as well. Similarly, earthquakes are very quick, medical emergencies, same thing. At risk of oversimplifying, the vast majority of the emergency itself is typically complete by the end of these first seven minutes.

Let's pivot for a moment to a wider-scale emergency to see how other pieces of proactive and responsive work can come together to build a safer community even as soon as the moments after the emergency began.

In Chapter 7, we discussed the principles of incident command, the concept that in order for any emergency to unfold meaningfully and correctly, we must have leadership and communication in place. The design of your incident command model is a proactive tool. You're going to be much better off in these first seven minutes if you've created the model and trained on it. So for anyone assigned to a team/role in the ICS chart, there should be additional training for them proactively. Just as everyone on campus should teach, drill, assess, the ICS team (which in some smaller schools, might wind up including everyone and in larger schools, might only include some staff/teachers), should do the same. On average, we're looking for about 1.5 hours of training—60 minutes at the beginning of the year and 30 minutes in January as a refresher—and we want to activate them during drills (more on this in the hours phase in the next chapter).

Your incident commander, for example, has the opportunity, typically within the first seven minutes, to get on the PA system and announce that there's a fire on campus in the art room and everyone must evacuate using the closest available exit. Or if there's a person on campus who doesn't belong (aka an intruder/shooter), they can get on the PA system and say, "Lockdown," or "Run, hide, fight," depending on the protocol and the behavior from the shooter.

Furthermore, your PIO, or public information officer (or director of communications), can get into the Emergency Notification System and process an emergency notification to be sent out to everyone's phone, email, laptop/projector/classroom monitor screens. It's critical to note that you don't normally have time in these seven minutes to wordsmith the message. So, instead, you need to have the templates loaded in the system proactively. At the end of the book, I offer templates that we use at Joffe Emergency Services that you can customize for your school/organization's needs (just scan the QR code).

There's a social construct that Amanda Ripley describes in her book *The Unthinkable* that relates to the government, and I want to connect it to what has become our shared work. "Trust is the basic building block of an effective warning system. Right now, it's too scarce in both directions: officials don't trust the public, and the public doesn't trust officials."[5] The net, here, is that we can fall for a trap. We don't trust people not to panic, so we don't communicate. In turn, they panic, because they don't trust us to communicate.

The first seven minutes provide the first opportunity to start dialogue with every stakeholder on campus and provide an opportunity to at least create ground rules for those in the greater community.

---

[5]Ripley, *The Unthinkable: Who Survives When Disaster Strikes—and Why*, Harmony/Rodale: Emmaus, PA, 2008.

In the first seven minutes, schools should be communicating via all means available to the people on campus with essentially four key points:

1. What is happening.
2. What do you need to do.
3. Who is helping.
4. When you'll communicate again.

Each of the templates you'll find at the end of this book are designed to help address those four points. Over time, more might become useful, so just as you review your risk assessment annually, you should review these communication templates annually and determine whether there are opportunities to develop further communication. Note that as of today, text messages cap at 160 characters, tweets at 280, and so on, so brevity is critical. At the beginning of the emergency, you simply may not have any more information to share than "Lockdown. If on campus, lockdown now. If off campus, stay away. We have notified the police and will provide an update in 30 minutes."

Let's deconstruct this message for the purposes of helping you to modify any templates you wish to create:

1. What is happening? Lockdown. They know what is happening and what to do. Good.
2. What do you need to do? They know what to do if they're on or off campus. If you have the space available, it's even better to include a reminder about what that means: "Locks, lights, out of sight," for example. People will argue with me about whether that should be the standard. At Joffe, we've developed the perspective that we should communicate the detail of what to do verbally to those on campus via the PA system instead of via text because we want to prioritize the additional messaging within the text character limit. You should debate that rigorously for your own community and

then decide on a strategy—the one you believe in most. We choose to provide off-campus instructions because so many of the campuses we work with have students and staff who leave for lunch, might be arriving at the start of the day, or have left already if it's toward the end of the day. This is a very general overview here, and I believe in it, but the reason I'm giving you these notes, too, is to help you construct your debate so that you can make the best choice for your community.

3. Who is helping? They know that they're not on their own. They know that police have been notified. Because of the training done, they have an awareness of what's going to happen next. They won't be surprised. They know that police will likely arrive quickly, they expect to hear helicopters overhead, and more.

4. Next steps: Everyone has an expectation for when they'll hear from you next. You **must** meet this expectation. If you suspect you may not be able to, delete that sentence or change the number. Communicating every 15 minutes is a great practice if it's safe to do so and you have the tools. But you must ensure you do what you say you will do in these moments. As we'll explore in the next chapter, your commitments during the emergency will be used against you in the court of public opinion (and possibly in a court of law).

The next question becomes whether you should communicate to everyone in your community (read: parents/guardians) in this first-round communication. There are two opposing arguments. Here is the basic construct for both arguments, and they are interrelated:

- If you **don't** communicate to your parents/guardians, your students will.
- If you **do** communicate to your parents/guardians, your students will.

Whether we like it or not, most of us (not all!) live in an ever-more connected world. A study by Stanford researchers, from 2022, reveals that a small percentage of seven-to-nine-year-olds have cell phones, approximately 25 percent of 11-year-olds have a cell phone, and nearly 100 percent of 16-year-olds have a cell phone.[6] This study was a fairly small sample size, but it seems anecdotally relevant across our schools' populations, too. The bottom line is that kids have means to communicate with families.

Let's make this problem worse: If you're a child and your school goes into lockdown (the data on this is not as discoverable as we'd like. For now, we've used a *Washington Post* assessment to construct this perspective). Based on their data, in the 2017–2018 school year, approximately 16 campuses would go into lockdown on any given day (and the *Post's* own tally exceeded 6,200 over the course of that year. (I realize that math doesn't quite match, but what you should expect based on the data is that there are substantially more lockdowns on non-typical days after a major emergency (like the Parkland Shooting in February of that year.)[7] Using a different database, we conclude that there were 89 school shootings in 2017–2018. So, rough math here, but $89/6,200 = 0.0144 = 1.44\%$ of the time a school went into lockdown it was due to an active shooter (perhaps less because it's unclear whether in the WaPo dataset they included run, hide, fight, or other responses for school lockdowns).[8] This is as good a time as any to recognize

---

[6]Sun, X., Haydel, K.F., Matheson, D., Desai, M., & Robinson, T.N. (2023), "Are mobile phone ownership and age of acquisition associated with child adjustment? A 5-year prospective study among low-income Latinx children," *Child Development* 94, 303–314, https://doi.org/10.1111/cdev.13851.

[7]Steven Rich, "School Lockdowns: How Many American Children Have Hidden from Gun Violence?" *Washington Post*, December 26, 2018, https://www.washington-post.com/graphics/2018/local/school-lockdowns-in-america/.

[8]National Center for Education Statistics, "Number of Casualties from Shootings at Public and Private Elementary and Secondary Schools, Number of School Shootings, and Number of Schools with Shootings, by Type of Casualty and Level of School: 2000–01 through 2020–21," n.d., https://nces.ed.gov/programs/digest/d21/tables/dt21_228.12.asp?current=yes.

that there are approximately 130,000 K–12 schools in the United States. It's difficult to drill down to the likelihood by a specific percentage because of the diffuse sources of data, so I won't do that here, but we can agree that it's a rare occurrence. Increasing, yes. Terrible, yes. There shouldn't be even one school shooting, agreed. More in the US than in other countries, absolutely. But it is in fact, rare.

For a variety of reasons, the data on gun violence is sparse and vigorously debated. Harvard School of Public Health shared, "One major reason for this lack of data is a 1996 Congressional budget rider called the Dickey Amendment. Named for its sponsor, Arkansas Republican Congressman Jay Dickey, the amendment forbade the US Centers for Disease Control and Prevention (CDC)—the agency charged with protecting America from health threats—to use funds for injury prevention and control "to advocate or promote gun control."[9] Whatever the backstory, fortunately, there's more research now than ever before and we still have a lot to unpack, understand, and explore.

I spell all of this out and provide the data in Figures 9.2 and 9.3 in large part to share this key point: It's highly unlikely that the lockdown we're experiencing any given day is the result of an active shooter. *But* a child doesn't know that. Not even a teacher knows that. Not even an on-campus security leader may know that at the beginning. So the message the child will send home is likely associated with a substantial fear they have, be it an active shooter, a kidnapping threat, or something else. Therefore, communication to home early and often enables parents to hear not just from their child but from you, too. Especially if it's a lockdown because of a police pursuit near campus, or a response designed to protect the community proactively.

Pro tip: It's a great practice to tell families at the start of each year how you'll communicate with them in emergency situations.

---

[9]"Why There's so Little Gun Violence Research," *Harvard News*, June 22, 2018, https://www.hsph.harvard.edu/news/hsph-in-the-news/gun-violence-research-dearth/.

Table 228.12. Number of casualties from shootings at public and private elementary and secondary schools, number of school shootings, and number of schools with shootings, by type of casualty and level of school: School years 2000-01 through 2021-22

School year	Number of casualties from shootings			Number of school shootings, by type of casualty				Number of schools with shootings, by level of school[1]				
	Total	Deaths	Injuries	Total	Number with deaths	Number with injuries only	Number with no casualties	Total	Elementary schools	Middle or junior high schools	High schools or other schools ending in grade 12	Other[2]
1	2	3	4	5	6	7	8	9	10	11	12	13
Total, 2000-01 through 2021-22	1,676	515	1,161	1,375	382	591	402	1,305	320	162	777	46
2000-01	47	18	29	30	16	7	7	30	4	3	23	0
2001-02	18	5	13	17	5	8	4	17	2	1	14	0
2002-03	29	13	16	24	12	7	5	24	2	6	16	0
2003-04	45	16	29	34	12	16	6	34	5	3	26	0
2004-05	63	22	41	44	12	27	5	44	9	1	32	2
2005-06	55	13	42	51	12	30	9	50	5	6	39	0
2006-07	91	28	63	64	21	35	8	64	9	12	42	1
2007-08	23	10	13	16	8	6	2	16	2	2	11	1
2008-09	61	19	42	52	19	22	11	52	11	6	31	4
2009-10	15	5	10	15	5	6	4	15	1	2	12	0
2010-11	32	8	24	18	7	10	1	18	4	2	12	0
2011-12	21	9	12	16	6	8	2	16	3	3	9	1
2012-13	55	42	13	26	14	8	4	26	7	5	13	1
2013-14	55	19	36	46	15	22	9	46	7	3	32	4
2014-15	65	20	45	43	15	20	8	43	13	4	24	2
2015-16	45	9	36	38	8	19	11	38	7	4	25	2
2016-17	61	14	47	48	13	26	9	48	8	9	31	0
2017-18	185	52	133	89	22	37	30	89	14	8	64	3
2018-19	116	34	82	115	33	45	37	113	35	14	60	4
2019-20	126	32	94	116	27	51	38	116	33	11	70	2
2020-21	118	46	72	146	43	50	53	145	59	21	57	8
2021-22	350	81	269	327	57	131	139	319	82	37	189	11

[1]Schools that had multiple shootings in a single year are counted only once in that year's total, and schools that had shootings in multiple years are counted only once in the total across years.

[2]Includes schools for which school-level information was unknown or unspecified as well as those whose school level was "other."

NOTE: "School shootings" include all incidents in which a gun is brandished or fired or a bullet hits school property for any reason, regardless of the number of victims (including zero), time, day of the week, or reason (e.g., planned attack, accidental, domestic violence, gang-related). Deaths and injuries include both shooters and victims. This table was created using a database that aims to compile information on school shootings from publicly available sources into a single comprehensive resource. For information on database methodology, see K-12 School Shooting Database: Research Methodology (https://www.chds.us/ssdb/resources/uploads/2020/09/CHDS-K12-SSDB-Research-Methods-Sept-2020.pdf). Due to adjustments made to the learning mode (in-person, remote, or hybrid) during the coronavirus pandemic, caution should be used when comparing data since 2019-20 with those from earlier years. Some data have been revised from previously published figures.

SOURCE: U.S. Department of Defense, Naval Postgraduate School, Center for Homeland Defense and Security, School Shooting Safety Compendium, internal data files. (This table was prepared September 2022.)

Figure 9.2: Number of casualties from shootings at public and private elementary and secondary schools, number of school shootings, and number of schools with shootings, by type of casualty and level of school: 2000–01 through 2020–21.[10]

I like to teach families using the "7s" so that they can understand that while we aspire to get messaging out immediately, it may take a few minutes—that way there's a bit of cover for the school if there are competing priorities (remember: physical safety is paramount). Furthermore, teaching, maybe even during this session, that you will use lockdowns for threats other than active shooters (if that's your protocol) can help calm nerves of anxious families.

---

[10]Data taken from the source National Center for Education Statistics, "Number of Casualties from Shootings at Public and Private Elementary and Secondary Schools, Number of School Shootings, and Number of Schools with Shootings, by Type of Casualty and Level of School: 2000–01 through 2020–21," n.d.

Table 105.50. Number of educational institutions, by level and control of institution: 2009-10 through 2019-20

Level and control of institution	2009-10	2010-11	2011-12	2012-13	2013-14	2014-15	2015-16	2016-17	2017-18	2018-19	2019-20
1	2	3	4	5	6	7	8	9	10	11	12
All institutions	**138,925**	---	**136,423**	---	**139,126**	---	**139,874**	---	**137,432**	---	**134,960**
Elementary and secondary schools	**132,183**	---	**129,189**	---	**131,890**	---	**132,853**	---	**130,930**	---	**128,961**
Prekindergarten, elementary, and middle	91,753	---	90,175	---	92,748	---	92,046	---	90,357	---	88,909
Secondary and high	26,904	---	26,524	---	26,724	---	27,144	---	26,962	---	27,155
Other, ungraded, and not applicable/not reported	13,526	---	12,490	---	12,419	---	13,663	---	13,611	---	12,897
Public schools	98,817	98,817	98,328	98,454	98,271	98,176	98,277	98,158	98,469	98,755	98,469
Prekindergarten, elementary, and middle	70,142	70,427	70,291	70,007	70,050	70,113	69,931	69,612	70,112	70,261	70,039
Secondary and high	23,499	23,728	23,195	23,348	23,311	23,441	23,472	23,379	23,318	23,567	23,529
Other, ungraded, and not applicable/not reported	5,176	4,662	4,842	5,099	4,910	4,622	4,874	5,167	5,039	4,927	4,901
Private schools	33,366	---	30,861	---	33,619	---	34,576	---	32,461	---	30,492
Prekindergarten, elementary, and middle	21,611	---	19,884	---	22,698	---	22,115	---	20,245	---	18,870
Schools with highest grade of kindergarten	5,577	---	4,883	---	5,515	---	5,411	---	4,585	---	4,328
Secondary and high	3,405	---	3,329	---	3,413	---	3,672	---	3,644	---	3,626
Other, ungraded, and not applicable/not reported	8,350	---	7,648	---	7,509	---	8,789	---	8,572	---	7,996

Figure 9.3: Number of educational institutions.[11]

[11] National Center for Education Statistics, "Number of Educational Institutions, by Level and Control of Institution: 2009–10 through 2019–20," n.d., https://nces.ed.gov/programs/digest/d21/tables/dt21_105.50.asp. / U.S. Department of Education / Public domain.

Before we can exit the seven minutes chapter, there are a few key myths, challenges, and common threads to address:

> Code words: After 9/11, the greater emergency preparedness community went toward using code words to suggest level of concern. In fact, you might even remember the national threat level "Red, Orange", etc. Generally, we've found that those are not effective at managing the community level of awareness and can create confusion, lack clarity, and in the words of Janet Napolitano, the Homeland Security Chief from 2009 to 2013, the DHS moved away from the terms because "the goal is to replace a system that communicates nothing," the agency said, "with a partnership approach with law enforcement, the private sector and the American public that provides specific, actionable information based on the latest intelligence."[12]

We run into something similar with code words used on campuses to initiate lockdown or communicate a threat. As of the time of writing this book, code words are deemed by the greater emergency management community as an ineffective way to communicate. In fact, you may have heard of the "10 codes" system that fire and police agencies used to use and largely even those agencies have moved away from them toward a mode of communication known as "plain language." Communication is about getting the message from point A to point B, and in general, the best way to do that is to use the words that do that. For all those reasons, in general, we opt against code words.

Code word proponents will cite one of two reasons to use them: (1) We don't want to create panic (if a student hears a word that means lockdown, that might be terrifying), (2) we don't want to tip off the intruder that we know they're there. Despite both reasons,

---

[12]Schwartz, John. "Color-Coded Terror Alerts to Be Dropped by Homeland Security," *The New York Times*, November 25, 2010, https://www.nytimes.com/2010/11/25/us/25colors.html.

both the I Love U Guys Foundation and Joffe Emergency Services have chosen to stay the course with direct communication.

For a quick rebuttal to those responses:

(1) We don't want to create panic: Of course, nobody wants to create panic. However, we want to be the catalyst for an organized, practiced response. Having talked in the previous chapter about the importance of drills, the reality is that whatever word you use is going to become known to the community during your drills. Therefore, students **will** in fact know the word, even if you've tried to obfuscate it. Therefore, you might as well use the plain language so that subs, parents, visitors, and others know the word. Moreover, if a student truly doesn't know the code word and they're in the bathroom, hallway, or otherwise without an adult, we've missed an opportunity to notify them of the concern.

(2) We don't want to tip off the intruder that we know they're there: As we discussed, most lockdowns do not involve an active shooter. In fact, often the situation is because police have chased someone onto or near campus, a weapon has been discovered, or other similar reason. In each of these cases, **including an active shooter,** the person (if involved) will glean from their surroundings that the school knows they're there. Using plain language helps people respond more quickly (get behind a closed and locked door, etc.), and there's no evidence to suggest that this changes the intent or motivation of the person (if involved) who's there to cause harm. Additionally, the US Government Accountability Office concluded that about half of shootings were committed by current or former students who would likely know the codewords anyway.

The issue of plain language vs. code words will come into question routinely after a major shooting occurs. I challenge you—and myself—to examine it regularly and transition strategy as appropriate.

800 Numbers

Many schools developed an 800 number around the same time as 9/11. The idea was that during 9/11 it was so difficult to get ahold of one another because phone lines were overwhelmed that schools chose to create and distribute an 800 number that families could dial into in order to get information about what was going on. This picked up steam at the same time as what we now know as Emergency Notification Systems (ENSs). ENSs are just more practical tools in that we can communicate proactively to families instead of relying on them to call into a number. For that reason, generally, we recommend ENSs over the 800 number. As is always the case, if you can have both, redundancy never hurts if you ensure they're both linked or kept up to date!

Role of Armed vs. Unarmed Security

Often people ask about the role of security during the first seven minutes of an emergency. I find that people seem equal parts enlightened and distraught when I talk about this, so I'll share a bit with you here. In general, unarmed school security does the same thing everyone else does in the event of a security-related emergency: They lock down or they run, hide, fight. If your security officer is unarmed, it's not wise for them to approach someone who is and try to stop the situation from escalating. We talk about the importance of getting to physical safety first for yourself and then those around you, and this also applies to your security officers! They must also put their own masks on before taking further action. Security might be aware of the threat earlier than anyone else if it's external (i.e. they may see someone walking toward campus with a gun) and therefore be able to be the first ones to sound the alarm, they should be supporting the evacuation process, engaging with police on arrival to provide known and relevant information, and so forth. Most importantly, unarmed security must not be relied upon to confront the shooter if this is an active shooter scenario.

Armed security is different in that they can be engaged to seek out and confront the shooter (and neutralize the threat), which is a nicer way of saying either disarm the person or kill them.

The critical reality to address here, though, is this: Even police, with all their training, expertise, and experience, only actually hit their target roughly one out of five times when they're taking fire themselves (about 50% of the time when not).[13] This data is based on police officers who generally experience a minimum of 664 hours (using the POST Training model). To become a licensed armed security officer in the same state as these police officers, there are roughly 40 hours of training required—less than 10% of what's required for police officers. (Of course, these numbers vary by state.)

The bottom line: If you're going to have armed security, you shouldn't rely exclusively on the security company's word or commitment to training. You should inspect what you expect. There are additional courses that you should send your officers to. You should ensure they have adequate range time to maintain proficiency, and you should ensure they're fully aware of their responsibilities and willing to and trained to perform their responsibilities in the event of an active shooter.

The Exception to Practice Makes Permanent

During drills the school leader will often do things like walk the hallways to make sure the doors are locked (in a lockdown drill), or check classrooms to ensure everyone has dropped, covered, and held (in an earthquake drill), or stand by the door reminding students to be quiet as they exit (during a fire drill). That's a great way for you to maintain leadership and engagement and to demonstrate your personal commitment to successful drills. That said, it can also set a dangerous precedent for your safety! Remember, during the real emergency, your job is to get to a place of physical safety for yourself first and those around you. I call this out because all too often, when we conduct tabletop exercises,

---

[13]Bernard Rostker et al., "Evaluation of the New York City Police Department Firearm Training and Firearm-Discharge Review Process," 2008, http://www.nyc.gov/html/nypd/downloads/pdf/public_information/RAND_FirearmEvaluation.pdf.

we find that leaders forget that they, too, need to participate in the physical safety steps. Please remember that your community needs you as part of the leadership process during and especially after the emergency is over (Table 9.2).

Table 9.2 Key lessons, steps, and roles.

Key lesson:	The first minutes of an emergency boil down to leadership and communication.
Key step:	Physical safety (again!)
Key roles:	
Teachers/staff:	Follow directions
Leaders:	Give directions
Students:	Follow directions
Parents:	Receive communication, but don't act yet. If off campus, sit on your hands. Stay out of the way. If on campus, follow directions.
Board:	Receive communication, but don't act yet. If off campus, sit on your hands. Stay out of the way. If on campus, follow directions.

10

Response
The First Seven Hours

During the first seven hours, your focus must be on:

- Maintaining physical safety;
- Proactive and reactive support for psychological safety;
- Communication with families;
- Reunification.

There are a few key realities of the first seven hours to consider:

1. You'll have completed, or largely completed the reunification process.
2. This is the opportunity to transition to recovery and rebuilding.
3. This is the opportunity to lean into leadership.
4. If the seven seconds and seven minutes weren't managed well, this is the last chance to take the crisis and turn it into a source of strength.

   Critical context: The biggest mental shift of the response will be the period from wrapping up the first day and breaking into the second day. It's a marathon, not a sprint. You'll go from climbing perhaps the biggest mountain of your life only to realize that you've only climbed up to the base of an entire mountain range. Don't go this alone. Build and rely on your team.

If you think back to the medical emergency we discussed in Chapter 9, the seizure in a classroom, you can imagine that there's little still to do here, at the seventh hour. You've communicated to families affected, you've gotten the student to follow on care, you've gotten through the bulk of the emergency. It is perhaps, then, true to imagine that the higher the percentage of people within the community affected, the longer you'll be managing the emergency. If the emergency is focused to the individual campus, (e.g. a power outage or a boil water warning, or plumbing back up), you might only get to seven hours. If it involves the entire neighborhood or affects the lives of students, it's more likely to extend to seven months or seven years.

Much of the work should have been done before the emergency takes place, but there are a few components to the hours portion that are fundamental to a successful crisis response. These will lay the groundwork for a recovery that you can continue to lead through. More succinctly: You'll maintain much of the confidence from your community, and you're less likely to be the leader for your community beyond the crisis.

In some cases, it's not right that the leader of the school is the one to take responsibility for what does and does not happen during the crisis. The reality, however, is that more and more since 2020, communities are looking at, and even blaming, the leader. An unsuccessful recovery or a higher-than-perceived-acceptable number of injuries (or worse), and the leader may be the person the community will blame. This is too complex an issue with too many moving parts to address holistically here, but I will expand on this over time in the accompanying website materials.

Up to this point, mistakes have been masked by urgency. Your mistakes in planning, preparing, and even in the initial response

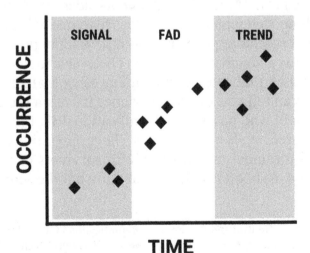

Figure 10.1: Occurrence vs. time.

aren't clear yet because the incident was still emerging. This is true of our longer-term, creeping crises, too. The initial moments (referenced in Figure 10.1 as weak signal) are just that—they're a weak signal of what's going on. Even frustration about the response will be masked by the lack of unity that exists at the onset.

The single greatest mistake that school leaders make as it relates to this portion of the emergency response is they don't practice with everyone involved. Let's examine another incident: We'll use a lockdown.

We had a school where a student was killed at dismissal time. It shouldn't surprise any school leader to hear that the greatest volume and often severity of emergencies will occur at dismissal, lunch, and arrival (typically in that order). The school had practiced, a lot, the steps required to initiate lockdown during the day (think about the 10:15 drill on Tuesdays). But the school had not yet conducted a reunification drill. Reunification might be a new concept for some of our readers, so let's examine what this is. The CDC's definition is importantly broad and includes not just school but other environments as well: "Reunification is the process of ensuring that children return to the care of their parent(s) and family as quickly as possible after an emergency."[1]

What's the greatest mistake our school leaders are making? Not doing nearly enough reunification drills. This is one of the processes/practices that is seldom practiced and if so, seldom practiced with actual students and parents. We haven't been able to find a reliable national data set that assesses how many schools are conducting these, but I can tell you in my experience if I ask a group of 100 heads of school who has done a reunification drill, I typically see just two or three hands raised. This is a *huge* opportunity.

First and foremost, when we talk to survivors of incidents, primarily active shooter incidents, about what the reunification

---

[1] Centers for Disease Control and Prevention. "Reunification | Caring for Children in a Disaster | CDC," January 6, 2021, https://www.cdc.gov/childrenindisasters/reunification.html#:~:text=What%20is%20Reunification%3F,as%20possible%20after%20an%20emergency.

process was like, we hear horror stories. For families who picked up their children, we hear the stories of rushing to the school and then being rerouted to another location—perhaps a fire station, a parking lot, or another campus. We hear stories of rushing to the school and being stuck, waiting outside campus, until they were authorized to go toward the reunification location. We've heard of people who feared that their children were hurt or worse, simply because information was not clear.

I've heard people reflect that because we will run reunification in a similar way to the way we run dismissal, practicing reunification isn't necessary. I argue that vehemently, because it's not going to be apparent, at least to families, how successful you were at search and rescue. You may save their child, but they will not see that take place. It is not readily apparent to families how successful you were at psychological first-aid. You may treat their child and stop trauma from becoming an exponential and lifelong disruption for this student, or mitigate the damage of a specific situation, but they will typically not see that. Therefore, they will struggle to fully understand or fully appreciate the reality of the work that is done in those areas.

They will not see assembly and attendance. They will not see first aid and triage. They won't see the incident commander, aside from the communication that takes place, where they're receiving information about what's going on or where to go, but they will see reunification. In fact, every emergency will end with reunification. **If we get reunification right, families are more likely to feel more comfortable dropping their children off the next day.** It's just a fact that the part of the experience that they will see has the greatest impact on their confidence in our school to keep their child safe. We have got to get reunification right.

In some cases, families arrive on campus or arrive at the reunification area and their student is not able to be released to them because their student has been hurt or worse. Often, in the events that we've observed over the last 20 years, we've found that, in those cases, while the parent is waiting at the reunification area, they've not been given the information that their student will not be released with the rest of the students.

Often, parents expressed that they experienced a process of elimination. One by one, other students are released while this parent is waiting for theirs. For those that have children, I can only imagine the pain, the suffering, the terror, and the fear that one must experience as you see child after child released, not to see your own, even in the distance. Society has to do better for these families.

Let's take a moment to discuss a shooting that occurred in Atlanta where nobody was killed, but we used the reunification process. The police department chose to use the reunification process and transport students from campus to a store's very large parking lot. They were transported in school buses and armed police officers stood by at the doors of the buses as parents waited to pick up their children.

The police officer walked up on the bus and said, "Which student is in the front row?" and brought that student down and said, "I have this student. Is the parent here?" The parent ran up. The police officer got onto the bus to get the second student. By the time the police officer turned around, they had been overwhelmed by parents who were rushing the bus, grabbing their children.

During and after an emergency, parents will do anything it takes to get to their children. This plays out during reunification. The lesson we must take into our planning is that our system needs to be transparent. It needs to be clear. It needs to be practiced. It needs to be fast. In the case of the parking lot reunification, the biggest opportunity for improvement would have been to conduct a reunification drill beforehand so that families had exposure to what the process would be like. We're training families in those drills as much as we're training teachers.

We had a school in Northern California that had conducted reunification drills three or four times in a row, year after year. Teachers and students were comfortable with what the reunification process would look and feel like. Both had practiced it. Families, even, were comfortable with what the reunification process would look and feel like, because yes, they had practiced it, too.

So when the school next door went into lockdown due to a specific situation that concerned only that school, and this school—our partner school—decided to initiate reunification, teachers, students, and families jumped right into the experience and the process that they had learned.

What we discovered in this moment is that we had trained parents as much as we had trained anybody else. In fact, in some cases, parents were giving tips to the teachers because they, in some cases, had been at school for four years, whereas some of the newer teachers had only been on campus for two or three. They offered tips such as, "If you stand here, you can see further down the road," or "If you grab my identification at the previous checkpoint, you'll be able to move this process more quickly." There was a partnership that existed between parents and teachers or parents and folks on the reunification team, simply because the practice was there, and they were able to call back on that prior experience to get the job of releasing students done and to do it in a way that was effective.

If you want to build a reunification team on your campus, look across your faculty and staff for folks who know a lot of families and a lot of students. In fact, this includes the people who are already on the daily dismissal team. If you have a rotation of teachers, a core team of security, or an admin rotation who participate in dismissal, start there.

If you have these resources, think about your admissions/recruitment team, who greeted, screened, and got to know families before they entered the community. Think about your specialists who know almost all your children. Think about your security guards, who inherently encounter most of your families as they enter campus. Think about your front desk folks, who, again, speak with families daily. Think about your health folks. If you have enough health folks available that you can have some on first-aid and some on reunification, they too are accustomed to dealing with students and families, especially our higher-needs students and families.

From there, you can adjust or add to the group whatever you see fit, with the idea that you want to get to a place where we have approximately 8–15 people on the reunification team.

> **Small-school tip:** If you don't have many faculty/staff members, you can combine teams. There's added context on this on the accompanying website, but at the very least consider making your search & rescue team the same group as your reunification team. In practice, you'll generally be done with search & rescue in the minutes following the catalyst, and reunification won't even begin until a bit later (especially in natural disasters). For more small-school tips, head to the website.

It starts with picking the team and finding ways to practice. There are multiple existing modalities for reunification. There's an argument that we should all align with one, and I tend to subscribe to that argument, which is the Standard Response Protocol that comes out of the I Love U Guys Foundation. There are also other tools that some police departments have created.

At Joffe, we have a vehicle-based reunification strategy that uses the same basic principles and processes as the Standard Response Protocol guidelines. The biggest difference is that it keeps people in vehicles where practical (e.g. earthquakes) so that we're more able to control where vehicles are parked and left.

In 2008, we had a substantial train crash take place in Chatsworth in Southern California. I wasn't there but have sat through numerous trainings that have been amended because of what we learned there. As all the fire department, police, and other personnel arrived, additional resources did, too. The additional resources wound up parked behind one another. The first responders who got there parked in the front. Then people who arrived second parked behind them. Then the people who got there third parked behind them, and so on.

The people who were in the front were first ready to pick up and carry patients away and inadvertently had become trapped because the vehicles that were behind them had been left and keys weren't available to move them. So we learned from an EMS perspective and a response perspective to navigate the entire response differently—to create a staging area where we would pull one ambulance in at a time as we were ready to transport a patient.

We need to consider that same strategy as we think about how families will rush to campus and, if given the opportunity, may leave their car, likely not their keys, and could create a traffic jam, especially for schools on a narrow or residential street.

The second thing to think about, when it comes to building a reunification team and process, is designing a practice model that makes sense for your school. The reunification process is not going to take much longer than a normal dismissal. So one of the practices that we are working to adopt within our partner schools is to do an annual reunification drill.

In an ideal world, every spring there's a reunification drill where most of the families at every school get to participate in the process. We have them arrive at school, perhaps at staggered times. They experience what it's like to receive a text message that tells them what to do and where to go. They experience what it's like to be given different directions than normal. They experience what it's like to navigate through multiple stations where they're checked, vetted, their students are brought to them, and then they're released.

They experience this because we know that after an emergency happens, people can fall back into the experiences that they've practiced. It's the core reason that we conduct drills. We teach people what to do when the fire alarm is pulled and when they hear gunshots because we ask them to then activate their muscle memory when the real emergency happens. With parents, we're doing the same thing. We're simply inviting them into our drill, and we're inviting them in to build muscle memory so that when an emergency happens, they have something to guide them other than, or in addition to, fear.

The reunification drill doesn't need to take hours. It can be simple. It can be straightforward. It can be simply a modified dismissal, or it can be coupled with a more full-scale exercise where other teams—like search and rescue, first aid, and crisis counseling—get to practice. But reunification is a critical part of every emergency (Table 10.1).

The basic commitment that we make to families when they drop off their children is that we are going to give their child back at the end of the day. And while that is, unfortunately, not a commitment that we can live up to 100 percent of the time, especially when we see acts of violence or forces of nature, we need to recognize the fact that all emergencies will inevitably end in reunification because we are honoring our commitment to as many families as we possibly can to give their children back.

So if the first difficulty is, ostensibly, parents, then the second difficulty of these hours becomes your board and other community stakeholders. You're likely noticing a trend here that the people on campus (at the center of the community—in fact, even those at the scene of the incident) are the sole focus in the first few moments of the crisis. Over time, however, we begin to expand that reach as the media arrives, as student conversation with

Table 10.1 Key lessons, steps, and roles.

Key lesson:	The first minutes of an emergency boil down to leadership and communication.
Key step:	Physical safety (again!)
Key roles:	
Teachers/staff:	Follow directions
Leaders:	Give direction
Students:	Follow directions
Parents:	Receive communication, but don't act yet. If off campus, sit on your hands. Stay out of the way. If on campus, follow directions.
Board:	Receive communication, but don't act yet. If off campus, sit on your hands. Stay out of the way. If on campus, follow directions.

parents continues, as life safety shifts from being the sole focus to the primary focus. Your objectives, however, remain the same:

We want everyone to:

1. Get into a position of physical safety for themselves and those around them;
2. Begin to contemplate psychological safety as practical;
3. Communicate;
4. Establish or fall in line with leadership.

11 Assessment
The Following Seven Days

As the emergency evolves from hours into days, we see a few key opportunities, challenges, and realities. Fundamentally, the emergency (probably) wasn't your fault. You (probably) didn't set the building on fire, cause a chemical spill, and so on. But what you'll do with that situation is proven out over the days that follow. You'll likely have experienced extreme or acute moments of stress, and hopefully, you or someone at school demonstrated phenomenal leadership. What you may not account for, however, is what will happen to your cell phone after the evening news runs (should it be an incident that is aired on the news) or what will happen after you send any announcement email to the community (read: press release).

Another critical reality that most school leaders don't anticipate—or at least don't really take advantage of—is the outpouring of support that comes in. Eileen Opatut, who had been a successful television programming executive, a successful realtor, and more, was looking to volunteer to help find deeper meaning in her life. About volunteering for a smaller organization that perhaps didn't, yet, have the infrastructure in place to fully take advantage of her support, she said, "I was there, I was willing to do anything needed to help, but they didn't really know how to use me." That's what countless members of the community will report after a major crisis. In fact, one job not accounted for above on the teams' structure is a dedicated assistant to the incident commander and a dedicated community support manager as soon as practical. Often, the public information officer (PIO) who is listed can transition to that role.

In a response to a major crisis (a school shooting, an explosion, or other such high-profile and life-threatening events) this role can be critically important, particularly when it comes to thinking about how to deploy people eager to help. The assistant will take the incident commander's cell phone and manage incoming calls, texts, and support from the early moments on. This person might take your phone in the minutes-to-hours phase and may even hold onto it at some points throughout the day. In the earliest moments after an event, you'll be inundated by family, friends, colleagues, and past students/community members asking questions and seeking ways to support. The mayor's office may call you, the head of the local food pantry might call, the governor may call, in some cases, especially the most difficult ones, you may even receive a call from the president. If you're outside the US, the same applies to you; however, you will likely not only receive calls from within your country but internationally, too, especially if you're at an international American School. I'm hovering here because there's a critical reality that you will be unequipped for if I don't. You need to get to a place where you can receive support. If you don't yet know what would be useful, you can simply say something like: "Mayor, I appreciate your call and your support, and I'm overwhelmed right now. I don't know yet how you can be supportive to our community, but I will have a better sense of things in the next twenty-four hours. Can we reconvene tomorrow to discuss?"

The perpetual demands for time, energy, and capacity will continue mightily through the day and through the night. One of the best ways to manage this is to ensure there is some support to manage your cell phone (literally, just to keep it charged, even) and that you have someone then managing your calendar so that the promises for further support can be managed.

As with many other topics we've discussed, there is an inverse to this problem: In a natural disaster where you're just among the people affected, the opposite might be true.

We often use the California earthquake of 1994 as an example. This is perhaps one of the most central tests of this book, and I hope it stands the test of time. I meet regularly with my colleagues at Caltech, Pasadena, where Dr. Lucy Jones, the most notable earthquake expert, built a career, a lab, and a perspective on earthquakes that for the first time (I'd argue) begins to make sense to the rest of the world.

> Dr. Lucy Jones is a brilliant seismologist who has crafted a seminal work on earthquakes, tectonic plates, and the like. She's built the basis upon which earthquake early warning

can be established, and she's reimagined the "magnitude" that was previously used and confused regarding the intensity of an earthquake, and while Harry Wood and Frank Neumann established the basis, I don't believe that most Americans heard the concepts around the Modified Mercalli Intensity Scale until Dr. Lucy Jones shook things up. She works alongside a woman named Margaret Vinci, who is not a scientist but in truth sits at the intersection between scientists and the general public. Margaret's genius is talking with regular people—you and me—about earthquakes and helping us catalyze our preparedness efforts, strategize our response, and truly revolutionize the way we think about external support. The two of their work together is remarkable and a model for partnerships in the future.

Among many lessons I've learned from Margaret, the reality is that after an earthquake, we're not going to get support for quite some time. Let's use the Northridge Earthquake as one example (used because it's still ranked as the single costliest earthquake disaster in US history): On January 17, 1994, at 4:31 a.m. PST, a magnitude 6.7 earthquake centered in Northridge struck the Southern California area. Known as the Northridge Earthquake, it caused at least 57 fatalities (a subsequent study put the death toll at 72, including heart attacks) and injured thousands.[1]

In a case like Northridge, which, as an important benchmark, was "only" a 6.7 on the Richter scale (the old mechanism for measuring earthquake severity), we saw widespread damage. For context, California is well overdue for an even larger earthquake and we're anticipating it in the weeks, months, and years to come. Why am I bombarding you with this information and causing your blood pressure to climb? Because it's another type of crisis that we have to be equipped for. Even if your school isn't in California, we're all subject to earthquakes from natural causes or even potentially human-induced earthquakes from fracking

[1]Marshall, Daniel, *Risk Management and Insurance Review* 2018, Vol. 21, No. 1, 73–116, doi:10.1111/rmir.12097.

and other similar activities. If not earthquakes, there are similar potential natural disasters that can impact our communities, such as floods, hurricanes, tornados, and tsunamis. I use earthquakes because as of the date of publishing this book, we can only get advanced warning on earthquakes of up to about one minute (in the best of circumstances). That means that earthquakes hold a high severity but a limited warning, and as we learned earlier, that creates a greater overall risk.

So in an earthquake or other natural disaster, we run the risk of being without support from the government, local agencies, and so forth, for a period. We currently negotiate this among the community, and even FEMA's documentation as of the date of publishing says, "You could be without help for at least 72 hours, or up to two weeks. Self-sufficiency during this time is key."[2] We expand this to one week as the starting point because too often across our schools, upon our arrival into the community, the reality is that they're just not equipped for the long haul.

So Then, What Does Long-haul Preparation Look Like?

Being prepared for the first seven days boils down to a few key categories. Do we have the right stuff, the right strategy, and the right communication?

We've got to have the "stuff" pre-positioned. What stuff? Food, water, sanitation supplies, and basic communication infrastructure (AM/FM radios, cell phone chargers, walkie-talkies and chargers, etc.). There's a list of additional items in the accompanying materials that will evolve over time to help you keep a running tally of what you really need. It's very difficult, if not impossible, to get these items after a major emergency has occurred.

[2]"Earthquake Safety Checklist—Fema.Gov," FEMA, 2017, https://www.fema.gov/sites/default/files/2020-07/fema_earthquake_earthquake-safety-checklist_110217.pdf.

If you're mid-emergency, you might come up with creative alternatives and in some cases, lives will depend on it, so my hope is that you're able to do so, but I'm giving you this list in order to help you get ahead, to build your cache.

Food, Water, Sanitation

These things are central and critical if humans are involved. We'll need people to have food and water and to have access to a restroom from the onset of the emergency until the last folks are picked up/released. In many schools' emergency supply cache, I find tuna and saltines which technically meets the need but creates other issues: How thirsty are you after you eat a saltine cracker? It's ideal to put items in the cache that are purpose-built for emergency consumption. Most of the emergency food vendors at this point have access to low-sodium, high-calorie bars that nobody would ever want to eat on a good day, but most would be willing to eat after an emergency. It's important that you consider your community realities as you're managing which food sources you'll pursue. If you're a kosher community, there are kosher vendors! Most schools have some form of allergies on campus, but there are plenty of options that don't include peanuts, dairy, or other common allergens. You'll want to take a moment to think about your community and then find a vendor whose options match your needs.

One other consideration is how to build this cache. It's expensive, undoubtedly, to build this up, and like your security team, you're hoping you'll never actually need it. To that end, I typically recommend making the purchases in as large a volume as you can afford but defaulting to progress here, too. Here's an example ordering strategy for a school with 500 people in the community (figure 400 students, 100 adults) that has limited resources:

Year 1: Buy 500 people's worth of food and water for one day.
Year 2: Buy 500 people's worth of food and water for a second day.
Year 3: Buy 500 people's worth of food and water for a third day.

Continue until you've established your seven-day mark. It's critical that you don't wait to build the budget up over the course of seven years to then make the purchase because you just don't know when the emergency may occur. Of note, as part of an annual checklist, this needs to be reevaluated every year, and food, water, and so forth that have expired or been opened need to be replaced.

Pro tip: I typically recommend donating the food and water to a homeless shelter or food pantry approximately six months before it expires (after, of course, you've ordered new food and water). They'll be incredibly grateful because good emergency food is high in calories and they'll be able to feed a lot of people with it. It's important to sync up on a rhythm with them in advance, though, to ensure they have enough time to use it before it expires.

Other supplies can vary by school. If you go to the accompanying website, you can get a copy of the current checklist from either FEMA or Joffe Emergency Services to build on your supply cache. In general, though, it's like a camping list: Once you have food and water managed, you'll go on to thinking about sanitation, shelter, games and activities, medications, and so forth.

Strategy Is an Interesting Dilemma

I've participated in seven-day recoveries after severe fires, including building or organizational damage or complete destruction, after fatalities, after shootings, and more. In general, I'm laying out the strategies that are most often true across them all. It's critical that, well, like every other part of this book, you adapt these general outlines for your specific community.

Returning to Community and Routine

During Covid-19, we found the importance of returning to routine and community. It was not a "return to normal," and in fact I spent a lot of time in March 2020 (when Covid first shifted the way we operated schools in the United States) asking people to use words other than *normal*. Instead of saying, "I want to go back to normal," I asked people to say, "I want to stop worrying about my health during every interaction," "I want to start hugging my friends and family members again," and so forth. It's so important that we get specific about what it is that we want so that we can then work to achieve that. Especially important as a leader of a community, you need to hear what it is that people are yearning for in order to even begin to contemplate how you'll work to put that in place.

In my experience with major fires, with buildings damaged by smoke, flames, or the firefighting effort itself the same is true. Most of all, students and teachers have yearned for a return to routine and to community.

Given this, I work to reestablish routine as quickly as practicable. Options for reestablishing routine are endless in a now-hybrid world: getting everyone on Zoom for 15 minutes per day to hear an update from the principal, coming to a local community center for people to begin to access supports provided by the community, having students and families begin to practice gratitude (more about this in a moment) at a specific time of day using a specific audience to thank, and so many more opportunities. Routine does not mean coming back to school. It means coming back to a program where we know and understand what's happening now, what's happening next, and conceive of what's happening later.

We can test this together quickly. Think back to the early days of Covid-19, and think about the moments you remember most. When I do this exercise with an audience in person, I ask people to raise their hands and share a memory. I typically hear things such as:

- I walked my dog relentlessly (to the point that the dog saw me coming with the leash and ran the other way).
- I started walking by myself every morning or every evening.
- I played cards with my family every night.

- We all ate dinner together every single night.
- I worked to feed my elderly neighbors.

My school leader groups typically didn't have the above luxuries and instead said:

- I joined a daily webinar or podcast to get more information.
- I crafted a daily email to tell my admin team what to expect.
- I joined a daily Zoom call to update my colleagues and get updates on what was to come.

If any of that resonates with you, it's because you, too, found routine, even at a time that *absolutely nothing* was normal.

Community becomes the deeper area of focus, and so it's important to work to establish a mechanism of community. Humans are inherently relational beings. We want to establish connection, bonds, reciprocal knowledge, attraction, communication, and more with one another. (Adapted from *Human Foundations of Management: Understanding the Homo Humanus*).[3] Schools, I argue, go a step further.

One school that I work with had burned down once before. It was at risk of burning down again due to a fast-moving brush fire. When the head of school thought about what to quickly grab and bring off campus (there were no students on campus at this point), she chose to grab portraits of the founders of the school. These became a symbol of the importance of community and the fact that the community was about the people—not about the place in which they gathered. The school didn't burn down the second time, but had it, the portraits would have been a foundational element to reestablishing community.

Similarly, that same head of school had the students draw out cards thanking the firefighters for working to protect the school. Obviously, students—especially those who had also been

---

[3]Melé, D., C. Cantón, and César González Cantón, *Human Foundations of Management: Understanding the Homo Humanus*, Springer, 2014.

displaced due to the evacuations underway—were not in a place to learn arithmetic, but they were able to reestablish not just routine, but community by working together to build a massive box of thank-you cards, which were then circulated to the firefighters and other responders after the emergency came to an end. Your community might need to take a different approach, but these are ideas to spark creativity for you.

> **Action item:** Hopefully you're reading this book *before*, or worst case *after*, an emergency occurs, not during. In that vein, take a moment to jot down on the back cover of this book a few ways in which you might inspire your students, staff, faculty, and families to reestablish community and routine while you're facing the seven days after an emergency has occurred. You don't want to have to brainstorm during the event itself.

During human-related incidents (stabbings, shootings, etc.), a lot of uncertainty can creep up for every person in the community. In the event of a focused event (a stabbing of one person on campus, for example), it's important to build confidence in the ability to resume a meaningfully safe environment at school, and you can do that by simply sharing photos as staff return to the building (obviously once any crime scene is managed, cleaned, and you're cleared to access the buildings). You might even record a video of the school leader walking through campus demonstrating the colorful walls and bulletin boards. When a scary event occurs on a campus, it can become highly scary to return to campus for adults and for students, so the opportunity is there to help people understand that the school itself isn't a scary place, and the sooner you can return physically to the building, the better. Moreover, the sooner you can have people return, even just to pick things up, the less time for fear time to build. This is *fundamentally different* in an active shooter situation or one in which there was widespread community trauma. To that end, you'll need to consult with child and adult trauma experts before managing a return to the buildings.

The final element of strategy is that you'll need counseling in place as you work through the seven days following an incident. Note that if it's an earthquake and students are still on campus a few days later, that only exacerbates the need for counseling, but you might not have external grief or trauma counselors available to support you.

> **Action item:** Find three to five trauma counseling organizations that are near you to have on speed dial. Don't just put them on speed dial on your phone, but call them, talk with them, consider inviting them to campus to tour and talk about their strategy, and then ensure that you truly can call upon them after a major incident occurs. In the more rural parts of the world, you might have to build a network of individuals. In general, I like to have dozens of counselors available because (1) we might need them all, and (2) they might not all be available when our emergency occurs.

Communication

By now, it can't surprise you that I'm harping on communication here, too. Communication is bound to be a central challenge in the first seven days. Depending on the scope of the emergency, there are likely to be media interviews, police interviews, counseling assessments and reassessments, and so many moving pieces regarding routine. For this reason, I argue that the most important thing to focus on in the seven days following an emergency is setting expectations and then holding to them.

School leaders can feel pressured to decide when to reopen buildings or determine when the homecoming dance will be rescheduled to. Being clear about your strategy for making decisions can sometimes be even more valuable than making the decision itself (within reason).

Laying out the inputs to the decision you'll make can be as valuable to the community, especially mid-crisis, as the decision itself (Table 11.1). It's important to know your community on this as there are some decisions that people just need to have made. One example is if families are largely working and struggle with childcare already, any decisions about school being open for child-care are critical so that families can make work arrangements around them.

Table 11.1 Key lessons, steps, and roles.

Key lesson:	The first days of an emergency boil down to leadership and communication.
Key step:	Psychological safety is the through-line.
Key roles:	
Teachers/staff:	Engage in bidirectional communication.
Leaders:	Engage in listening, providing concrete structure for ongoing communication.
Students:	Engage in psychological safety building (counseling, high-trust communication, etc.).
Parents:	Receive communication, engage and provide meaningful feedback.
Board:	Receive communication, show up to support, engage meaningfully, stay in your lane. Do what's asked of you by the school. Ask your head what's not being asked of you and why.

I often encourage schools to start daily communication during crises. In and of itself, it's an opportunity to restore routine and begin to set and manage expectations. A letter might read something like this:

Dear community,

As you know, we're working to reopen school as safely and swiftly as we can.

Right now, we're working with smoke, fire, and debris experts to help us decide on when and how we can welcome students back to our building(s).

I had a chance to visit campus with our local firefighters today, and here's a picture of our front office: look at how resilient our school has been!

For the next 5 days, you can expect a daily email from me with an update on how we're doing in getting our school ready for our students and teachers to return. In the meantime, if you have the time wherever you might be, I want to ask you to help me thank the firefighters by making some thank-you cards at home. I'll let you know how we're going to collect them so that we can bring them to the fire station. I can't wait to see you again soon. In the meantime, you can always reach me by email!

Principal

12 Recovery
The Following Seven Weeks

The weeks following a major emergency are fraught with second-guessing, wondering, reanalyzing, overanalyzing, and frankly, your own trauma. Too often, as school leaders, we forget that we experienced the crisis, too.

In March 2020, at the beginning of the Covid-19 response in the United States, I said, "The biggest threat to our communities isn't the virus itself but the impact it will have on our leaders." I said a lot of things at the beginning of the pandemic, but I think that was one of the most important sentences, and it became the guiding light for the crisis work I do every day. I think it applies, though, to situations well beyond the pandemic. I'm *not* suggesting that the emergency itself isn't the problem: It is. Countless lives were lost in the early days of the pandemic, and lives are still being lost as of the date of publication of this book. But when we assess which communities endure—or even thrive—after an emergency compared with those that don't, I think the most successful are the ones who stay committed to a sustainable response from the start.

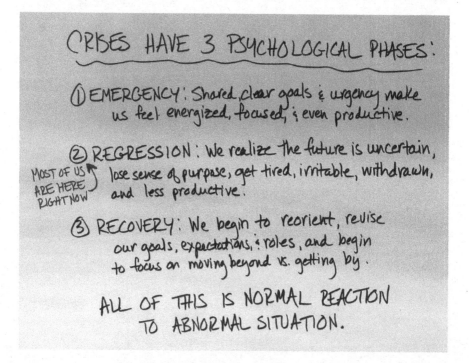

Figure 12.1: Psychological phases of a crisis.

Amy Cuddy, a social psychologist, delivered a similar image and perspective.[1] This aligns with the outline that we've already begun to talk about. The timeframe was different in Covid because of the widespread nature of the emergency and the ubiquity of its inherent disruption, but the phases were very similar to those we were experiencing then (Figure 12.1). In the first minutes to hours and often even days, we're galvanized by the emergency response. We have objective and clear goals (physical safety, psychological safety, etc.), and we are energized to accomplish them. What's more? Our cortisol levels are through the roof, and our physiological stress reaction is working for us and helping us to manage essentially every bodily function (our body is so good at this that it can make us forget we need to use the restroom for extended periods of time).

This transition into the weeks is the regression. Our cortisol hangovers kick in, and as leaders, we find ourselves in a sea of self-doubt. Did I do the right thing? Could I have done more? Our future becomes uncertain; our purpose becomes less clear and objective. I get it, I've been there too, all too many times.

Ingredients for recovery

You keep showing up. We'll keep mapping out the road ahead

Community working to support each other, and build the new normal we love

Goal + Pathway + Agency = Hope

Resume in-person education when it's safe to do so

The strength gained from uniting with others around this purpose

Figure 12.2: Ingredients for recovery.

[1]Cuddy, Amy and Jill Ellyn Riley, "Why This Stage of the Pandemic Makes Us so Anxious," *Washington Post*, August 11, 2021, https://www.washingtonpost.com/outlook/2021/08/11/pandemic-anxiety-psychology-delta/.

At the beginning of Covid-19's response in the US, Joffe created the visual in Figure 12.2 based on a concept shared by Brené Brown and repurposed it to focus on the inner workings of Covid-19. But I would argue that this can be extrapolated to any crisis in any locale. The concept is straightforward, but the execution of this methodology is painfully difficult and can be full of limitations and difficulties. Let's start by breaking down the concepts, and we'll then look at them via the lens of a few different types of crises.

Goal

Invariably, you've set goals before. You probably have a system in place that you use for this within your academic and even professional development programs. You should use that framework as a starting place. You may have some qualifier statements tied in and/or incorporate some strategies around how you'll execute on the goal safely. I've crafted a few of these over the years for varying crises and offer some starting points below.

In a fire recovery: Return to community, then, when safe, return to buildings, and then return to learning.

In a hurricane recovery: Engage in a community-wide effort to re-home every family who needs it.

In nearly any recovery: Build support for our community from our community.

The bottom line is that you need to reestablish a North Star because your primary goal, educating children through a rigorous curriculum in a diverse community, isn't going to work for the next few days, weeks, or months, so you'll need to have a more focused goal within arm's reach before you can return to the mission of the organization.

One of the most brilliant ideas that ever came up in the community recovery world was a self-sufficiency tracker (Figure 12.3). Jeanne, a former consultant at Joffe Emergency Services, put together a spreadsheet for a school she was working with through a crisis to help the community become self-sufficient. The spreadsheet was so simple and so straightforward that even a person

Point of contact name:	Point of contact email:	Point of contact phone:	What resource(s) do you need?	What resource(s) do you have to offer?	Notes:

During this event, our community is coming together to support eachother. Please use this spreadsheet to list support you need and/or support you have to offer. Doing so will enable others to see and reach out.

Figure 12.3: Community Self-Sufficiency Tool.

in crisis could complete it. Using this simple strategy, Jeanne managed to get food, childcare, vehicles, workspace, and other items distributed throughout a single school community. We began to refer to this as the Community Self-Sufficiency Tool, and we use it to this day (modified slightly during Covid to account for social distancing) during every single major community disruption.

Here are some basic questions (think of these as columns on an Excel sheet) to start:

- What resources can you offer?
- What resources do you need?
- Name;
- Phone number;
- Email address;
- Notes.

Why is self-sufficiency so important? When it comes to recovering from large-scale emergencies, no one person (or even group of people) can do it all. In the first seven seconds or minutes you don't have time to process all that you can't do. In the first seven days, you're so overwhelmed with the crisis itself and response and support that often you can't get to it then, either. This jump into the weeks, however, begins to reflect the gaps. Your own mental health and well-being will be challenged as the emergency fades. This is, again, a recognition of the regression in the greater community's response, too. Your cortisol levels dwindle, the excessive amounts of dopamine (the happiness hormone which accompanies cortisol in stress reactions) wanes, and it's more important than ever before to surround yourself with community.

You now know this, but your community doesn't, and so the next challenge (as I think often is the case for leaders) is setting the boundaries of what will and will not happen (the pathway).

Creating the Recovery Pathway

Here, the work is to outline the basic strategies you'll use so that the community can see how the work can be done. It's generally wise to keep the pathway wide because throughout the recovery, things will change, but you want to give people a sense for your vision of how it will unfold. In other words, you may use phrases such as "We want to come back to campus as soon as it's safe to do so. Today, based on the information we have, we think that'll be 8 days or so" instead of saying "We're coming back on the 29th" because things will inevitably change."

In the early days of the Covid response (roughly March 2020 through April 2021), I was running webinars for about 2,000 schools and used that as a platform to help schools, overall, work on the recovery process. In those webinars, we made the pathway very broad for the national audience we were working with at the time. We said, "You keep showing up, we'll keep mapping out the road ahead." This was a partnership. We weren't going to map things out for an empty (virtual) room, and they weren't going to show up unless we mapped things out. The flipside was that in Covid, we were mapping things out about 25–36 hours ahead of time, so we needed to be very clear that we wouldn't be getting further ahead for a while (at least in those early days).

In other events, though, the pathway is equally critical. What are the boundaries for the circumstance that you've encountered?

During a boil water notice (remember, not everything is a world-wide crisis), we might say, "We're going to hold school and use water bottles students bring from home."

The intent of your pathway is to ensure that everyone is on the same page and frankly, to help focus the group on achieving a goal and continuing along a set sequence. The sooner we return to routine, the better for students and adults alike, so that may well be a part of the pathway.

In the weeks phase, one caution is that the pathway, just like the goals you choose, are important to hold firm on. Yes, they may have to change if the overall emergency changes, but in this case, you're managing a critical emergency where people's psychological well-being is already in jeopardy (at best), and you may have students being released from the hospital. These weeks are highly stressful times to manage and experience, and the less you have to change about your path forward, the more confidence you'll create.

A consideration for all school leaders is to think back to the last time you were trying to raise money. Think back to how you managed to generate enthusiasm and buzz within the community—did you build a thermometer on the wall that ticked off the new donations made? Did you send a weekly email? Did you do an all-school assembly? These are some of the same vehicles you might consider using for your post-crisis pathways. You might consider a large poster outside your office that shows the three-week return strategy or a weekly (or daily) email that demonstrates the plan for getting kids back on campus along with the strategy to get counselors back. The reality is that, like so many other things we've talked about, you already have the tools. Our collective challenge is simply to make sure we're seeing them as tools, internalizing their lessons, and finding ways to apply them to any crisis we might face.

Agency

In our Covid example earlier, we said that the agency we needed from folks was the strength gained from uniting with others around a shared purpose. In a paper in 2016, James Moore referred to agency as "the feeling of control over actions and their consequences."[2]

Agency in crisis, or in recovery, is built on a bedrock of good, clear communication, high confidence, psychological safety, and good training. That is to say that people know what is expected of them, believe they can meet these expectations, and ideally can see the results of performance over time. A teacher, for example, might feel a lack of agency (they might voice it as helplessness) when it comes to talking with the family of a student who was in a fight. If your process on campus is that the dean takes over, that might be the case—the teacher might have no role or responsibility in the situation. But imagine that same teacher being trained on what the core steps were: (1) interview the students involved, (2) contact students' guardians and ask what happened and what might be going on, (3) make a discipline decision, (4) make appeals available through the vice principal's office. That same teacher can now walk parents through the steps (if allowed) and is now jumping from a passive role into an active role. They still are not involved in the process itself (at least as I've outlined it above), but they're engaged in the process strengthening their relationship with the family and creating a sense of agency and belonging.

I'm a huge advocate for teacher engagement largely because when I'm on campuses, delivering training, I hear a lot of the "we vs. they" or "teachers vs. administrators" conversations emerge, and I believe that the strategy to mitigate this is engagement (not lecturing, but engaging faculty as a part of the solution). I believe that's the case during the emergency, too, though. If you haven't yet created agency by involving teachers in designing the recovery process, a crisis presents an opportunity to do so, asking teachers to opt in to returning to school, involving them in the decision-making process for reentry, and so forth. I'm not suggesting that you do the entire recovery by committee, but you can create some opportunities for co-creation that enable everyone to participate,

[2]James E. Moore, "What Is the Sense of Agency and Why Does It Matter?" *Frontiers in Psychology* 7 (August 29, 2016), https://doi.org/10.3389/fpsyg.2016.01272.

buy in, and ultimately, feel safer as a result. The best examples are things such as cocreating the schedule for the first three days back on campus or cocreating the arrival procedure so that there are numerous adults in and around the carline.

After an isolated on/near campus shooting takes place (that is, a single student is involved and a non-student is the perpetrator), schools often engage me and my team to help facilitate the recovery process. In those cases, we generally use this agenda for the staff meeting. Obviously, there are many confounding variables, and it's critical to purpose-build any agenda or meeting for the situation. Generally, though, I use this as a reentry opportunity after a major event. This might be the first meeting of faculty and staff as they return to school for the first time in the days after the event:

1. Restore psychological safety:
   a. Review of the facts and rumor squashing.
   b. Ask how people are feeling, doing, and processing (this takes a while, and we don't cut it off).
2. Set ground rules:
   a. Over the next X days, we're going to need excellent communication because we have goals, which we'll outline in a moment, but they're ambitious and you are our priority.
3. Define the goal:
   a. We want to get students back on campus as quickly as possible.
4. Set the pathway:
   a. We're going to do some follow-up training today. Naturally, the question has come up: What if this had been worse? There's fear in the team that needs an outlet, and this is the opportunity to harness, focus, and maybe even reduce some of it.
      i. Training:
         1. Fire response (to reorient people to emergency training in a lighter, more accessible framework);
         2. Active shooter/lockdown response;
         3. Post-crisis response and support;
         4. Threat responses (more on this in a moment).

5. Establish agency:
   a. Our ask of you is that you will share with us how you're doing. We're cocreating the days ahead. We have a framework, but we'll adjust based on direct and indirect feedback from you. When my team is there, we have people give us a nod, a whisper in a hallway, or some other form of connection.
6. Define next steps:
   a. We're going to be here for the next X days without students to prepare for students to come back.
   b. We're going to do a daily email for the next Y days and want to invite your genuine responses.
7. Close the meeting with a recap, and then stay in the room for one-on-one conversation.

I mention threat responses above because they frequently come up after a shooting or other incident. In fact, sometimes they even are generated by off-campus events: Parkland, for example. In the days following the Parkland shooting in 2018, the Educators School Safety Network recorded about 50 threats per day, throughout the US, five times the "normal" volume of threats.[3] And because threats are not always reported effectively—or at all—that number may very well have been even higher than the dataset reveals.

The other side of the coin, however, is that threats enable everyone (staff, students, families) to shift from a passive to an active role in safety—they build agency. They're disruptive and upsetting and sometimes downright scary. And, real, perceived, or false threats all need to be taken seriously because we just never know which ones are legitimate. Running a compilation of real and false threats through our processes, however, enables us to

---

[3]McCallister, Doreen, "Threats Against Schools Increase Since Florida Shooting," NPR, February 22, 2018, https://www.npr.org/sections/thetwo-way/2018/02/22/587832544/threats-against-schools-increase-since-florida-shooting.

Table 12.1 Key lessons, steps, and roles.

Key lesson:	The first weeks after an emergency boil down to leadership and communication.
Key step:	Focus on psychological safety.
Key roles:	
Teachers/staff:	Engage in bidirectional, psychologically safe communication.
Leaders:	Engage in listening, build the pathway.
Students:	Engage in psychological safety building (counseling, high-trust communication, etc.).
Parents:	Receive communication, engage and provide meaningful feedback.
Board:	Receive communication, show up to support, free up financial resources to support your leader.

leverage our systems, training, and agency to act. Even threats that turn out to be unfounded become proof points that our systems are working (Table 12.1).

I like to use these weeks (or days if we get back to school more quickly) to teach folks about the importance of reporting threats and then to walk them through how to process and manage them to keep the community safe. It's basic stuff and work that you've likely already done with either your threat assessment team or your safety committee, so you have items to pull from, but it gives people a purpose to hold onto, and that can be a very useful tool to restoring agency, which can restore confidence over time.

13

Rebuilding
The Following Seven Months

The beauty of the months that follow a crisis is that earlier actions have begun to create a flywheel. Your progress creates a feeling of safety, which in turn creates increased confidence, which in turn promotes connection and engagement, which in turn creates physical safety. I don't want to overlook the difficulty of this period, though. Because, even a beautifully executed crisis response will be one of the hardest moments of your career and will take *almost* everything out of you in order to endure.

The hope of writing this book is that more and more school leaders will be able to confidently navigate a crisis response.

Joffe Emergency Services has always focused on creating a team that was "Useful. Expert. Curious." If you notice the dissonance between expert and curious, you did exactly what I wanted my team to do. To bring their expertise to the table, while also understanding that in emergencies (and, frankly, in life) things evolve quickly, there's always more to learn and do, and there's never a point when anything is completely finished. Seven months later, people may still be suffering from traumatic memories, buildings may still be closed or damaged, members of the community might remain only in people's memories. Useful, expert, and curious means we're able to adapt to support what's needed in the moment, at every moment, while sharing our own wisdom and learning from that of others.

Not all schools will create a crisis mission during an event, and not all schools probably need to, but especially for newer leaders, it can provide important grounding for how you'll process information and how you'll manage smaller decisions. Your school's culture and preexisting mission statement is a guiding light and, if documented, might even give you the foundation to work from.

There are a few recurrent challenges that occur in the months following a major emergency, and these are hard to manage. While not always the case, we've often seen that seven months after an emergency, people outside your community have moved on. The local news cycle lasts a few days for a major event in your community and a few weeks if there are major implications. A common (and rather depressing) term used in journalism is "if it bleeds, it leads." News outlets are trying to capture and keep people's attention, and big events at schools typically hold people's attention because they make us all feel vulnerable. Over the course of those early days, you'll be bombarded with calls and offers of support, but as the days turn into weeks and certainly as the weeks turn into months, that will shift. It will begin to feel, especially to students, as if the world has moved on from an event that was deeply personal to them. Students, especially adolescents, are already operating with a worldview that is different from adults; they haven't realized how big—nor how small—the world really is yet.

A few things may come of this. Students may seek further attention from the media and others. TikTok, Instagram, the five o'clock news, and so forth, might all be venues for students who are seeking a podium to find one and to share a perspective or reignite passion from the city, county, state, or even the world. Invariably, you'll have some students who continue this focus and other students who want to "return to normal," which is a phrase that I use only because I suspect you'll hear some students use it. You'll also have other students who will say, "We'll never return to normal."

This challenge warrants in-the-moment consultation with three key partners:

1. Student government / student leadership group(s);
2. Parent association;
3. School leader network.

The student government is probably obvious, but in short, you'll want them to be a part of the conversation, and maybe more importantly, you'll want to be invited to be a part of the conversation with them. For them, you'll need to show up as a leader and also a partner. You get veto power on one or two ideas, but you can't veto everything, or you'll be uninvited.

The parent association is similar. You'll want to be invited, though with parents, you can also do that by setting a meeting.

Parents have an added social pressure and are generally more likely to show up to a meeting you call than students are. For them, you'll have a bit more veto power, but you should really think of your role as channeling the students' asks to them and reinforcing the veto power you may have asserted to students.

Your network of school leaders is a different group altogether. This refers to any group of principals or leaders that can provide support and understanding. There is a group called the Principals' Recovery Network established by current and former principals of schools where a shooting has occurred. They are perhaps the most knowing resource you can reach out to for support, guidance, and care. It's likely that they'll reach out to you in the event of an active shooter situation. If your crisis was not an active shooter, then you may consider other principals or heads in your region, or call the state associations to get plugged in. **The action item buried within this is: Go build your network today, before an event occurs so that you have the group on speed dial, and you have relationships established up front.**

Implementing Progress/Learnings

It's critical that you make meaningful change as a result of the learnings from any given crisis. Typically, those changes will be manifested in documents such as your handbooks, your training materials, HR plans and hiring strategies, vision and mission statements (at times), and even commitments from individual stakeholders in your community. For example, after the Columbine shooting in 1999, Frank DeAngelis, then principal, committed to retiring from Columbine High School. He did, in fact, just a few years ago. His commitment to enduring leadership was demonstrative of his love for the community, his loyalty to the community, and his desire to cause the community to once again thrive. These are the types of commitments that are perhaps premature up until this point, but as you transcend from the weeks of crisis response

Table 13.1 Key lessons, steps, and roles.

Key lesson:	The first months after an emergency are going to have remnants of the emergency.
Key step:	Focus on psychological safety & rebuilding confidence and trust within the community.
Key roles:	
Teachers/staff:	Return to teaching.
Leaders:	Engage in listening, build the pathway.
Students:	Return to learning!
Parents:	Ask questions, be curious, but let your child pace the recovery.
Board:	Support your leader.

into the strategic crisis recovery, there becomes an opportunity to explore and adopt commitments along these lines (Table 13.1).

The Media

The media attention may come back periodically. Schools are cyclical, and so there will be routine reminders to the community at school and the community at large. Often, those will be at least:

- Returning from the next break;
- As students return the next school year;
- On the memorial date (the date the event occurred or the date the school returned, in some cases);
- When other events occur within the school or within the community.

As I was working on this book, there was a shooting at Michigan State University. The day students returned, MSU posted this well-crafted tweet acknowledging the media's right to be present (where allowed) and students' right to speak, while simultaneously managing the reality that not all students wish to speak to the media:

> *MEDIA ADVISORY: As students return to class today, we ask the media to please respect students' privacy and honor their choice on whether or not to be interviewed. We have received numerous complaints from students this morning feeling uncomfortable while walking to class.*[1]

A student who endured the Parkland shooting who has become a mentor and friend to me shared with me that she felt used by the media. The frequent calls when another shooting occurred or revisiting campus on specific dates and times left her feeling used and devalued. It's important to include these realities and choices throughout the evolution of the crisis response so that students, staff, families, and so forth, know and understand your expectations.

---

[1]MSU Police and Public Safety [@msupolice], "MEDIA ADVISORY: As Students Return to Class Today, We Ask the Media to Please Respect Students' Privacy and Honor Their Choice on Whether or Not to Be Interviewed. We Have Received Numerous Complaints from Students This Morning Feeling Uncomfortable While Walking to Class.," Twitter, February 20, 2022, https://twitter.com/msupolice/status/1627675898945368065.

14 Restoration
*The Following
Seven Years*

The final milestone to note is that years later, the crisis—and its subsequent response—will be woven into the fabric of the community's history. It has the potential to provide a source of future resilience, a set of values typically deeply tied into human connection, and it creates a community of students, teachers, staff, families, and others who will be forever shaped by it. Students may be transformed into activists, lives may be lost, and lives will be changed. When you reflect, after having moved through the phases of crisis, you'll likely find that in your own life there will be markers that remind you of the event.

I have experienced this myself. When I drive around Southern California I still point out corners where I picked up a patient overdosing on heroin, saw a horrifying car accident, found a man hanging from a tree, and more.

The greatest lesson, then, is that crises are in some way never complete. Sure, the early days of panic, denial, fight or flight will come and go, but in some profound ways, the crisis will persist or at least the outcomes of the crisis can persist to cause change, progress, or meaning.

To that end, I often talk with school leaders about a few principles that should exist well into the seven-year mark of the crisis. I'll share those with you here along with some asks and action items that you can leverage from the beginning until your time with that school comes to an end.

A Grade Span Is a Lifetime in K–12

If your school serves students in grades K–12, you'll still have students on campus who experienced the crisis for 12 years following the crisis. That's triple[1] the average tenure of a public school principal and double[2] the average tenure of an independent

---

[1]Guthery, Sarah, and Lauren P. Bailes, "Building Experience and Retention: The Influence of Principal Tenure on Teacher Retention Rates," *Journal of Educational Administration*, May 9, 2022, https://doi.org/10.1108/jea-09-2021-0172.

[2]"Headship Tenure," Head of School Database (HSDB), n.d., https://www.headsearch.org/tenure.html#:~:text=The%20average%20tenure%20for%20independent,after%20three%20years%20or%20less.

school head. It's highly likely that the evolution of the leader will outpace the evolution of a school and increasingly likely the more grades are served. Given this, it's important to ensure that community healing continues well beyond the departure of the crisis time leader. The next leader may be someone from within the community who experienced the crisis, too, but is likely not from within the community. If this is you, don't overdo it. Let the community guide the recovery process, but make sure you provide a space and venue to do so. You might have a school counselor or a local child trauma expert help you evaluate the impact of future drills, parent meetings, high stakes events, or other key opportunities for crises to emerge.

Restoration Is Not Replacement

As will be the case in the physical plant components of recovery, you'll never replace the days, weeks, or months of lost learning, lost time, or lost lives. Don't try. Instead, work to restore the social and emotional fabric of the community through acknowledgment of what's been taken and ownership for what you can do. Make promises you can keep, and *never* break them. I seldom use the words "always" or "never," but in this case it's important to use the word "never."

Cyclical Orgs Will Renew Trauma Cyclically

By their very nature, schools are cyclical organizations full of annual traditions, memories, and events. If a major event occurred on homecoming night, it will forever be remembered as the homecoming fire—or develop some other moniker—and it's important to weave those real memories into the curriculum, event-planning process, and conversation. Pretending as though we've forgotten is a mistake. Actually, forgetting could be unforgivable. Lean into the discomfort to ensure you're providing space for families, students, and staff who will be hovering in the discomfort.

Schools Are Learning Organizations That Promote Discovery

By their nature, schools promote experimentation, leveraging lessons learned, and reflection. That included learning through trial and error at times. Emergencies require this! Even in the most painful circumstances there are lessons that can be learned. Arguably, especially in those circumstances. Often, we find victims' families yearn for lessons to be learned to mitigate the risk of their pain being felt by another family. Paradoxically, schools often want to withhold any acknowledgment of mistakes in order to not cause pain to families. There are legal implications that must be considered with your school or district's attorney. But it's important to name that sometimes our driver is actually in conflict with the desire of those most severely impacted.

The Legal System Takes Time

In some cases, the perpetrator of the event—especially active shooters—will be on trial years later. We watched the trial of the Parkland shooter in 2022, four years after the event. For many families, the opportunity to heal didn't begin until the shooter was found guilty and sentenced to life in prison. The reality is that for some, healing is still on hold pending appeals. This is wholly unfair. In some cases, the survivors don't survive.

Too often survivors of critical community events attempt or complete suicide after the event. This includes their families and the responders who tried to help. There is a dearth of data on post-event suicide and loss. It's now being explored more rigorously, and I believe the findings will offer strategies to help victims, survivors, families, responders, and others cope with the aftereffects of these tragedies. In many cases after these events, I see the grief counselors pack up and go home after about 30 days. As the chapter title indicates, nearly every crisis is a years-long recovery process, not simply days, weeks, or months (Table 14.1).

Table 14.1 Key lessons, steps, and roles.

Key lesson:	Healing happens, forgetting doesn't.
Key step:	Interweave healing and community connectedness into the fabric of the recovery.
Key roles:	
Teachers/staff:	Teach, love, care! This is the moment to return to doing what we do in schools.
Leaders:	Prioritize remembering the event(s) at times of leadership transition.
Students:	Learn! This is the moment to return to doing what we do in schools.
Parents:	Seek continuous improvement in safety measures.
Board:	Prioritize remembering the event(s) at times of leadership transition.

Conclusion

The Obstacles to the Job Are the Job

Throughout this book, I've offered lessons and principles that I've learned over the course of the last decade from my work in schools and event venues. There's one final lesson that, strangely, started with my mom and translated over time to a shop owner in Puerto Rico.

I went to Puerto Rico with a group of students that were, like me at the time, getting their master's degree in design, business, and technology. The trip was considered one of these practical residencies where you get out for a week or two, learn about a specific company, area, or project, and then work on that thing. The idea is that you deliver a finished project or a finished product to the community that you're serving in whatever way you might be serving them.

I had chosen the Puerto Rico residency because it seemed like the most interesting and certainly had the most fun bar scene. More importantly, however, the location had the added layer of having experienced a hurricane several years prior. In 2017, Hurricane Maria hit Puerto Rico, and one of the things that was particularly challenging was it had followed Hurricane Irma, and the community was devastated. Many of us in the United States remember watching on TV and observing the difficulties that the community experienced with power, communication, food supply, and medical aid. The communication was so badly devastated during the early days of their recovery that many folks in the United States were unable to communicate with their loved ones in Puerto Rico.

We went as a group of about 20 or so USC master's students, ranging in age from early 20s to mid-40s. The very first day that I got there, I realized that I was going to fall in love with this island. We visited several remarkable towns and communities. I met people who demonstrated, even in lines at the airport, a sense of resilience that I've never seen in my life.

I was shocked at how patient people were when I offered my best version of "Buenos días," or any number of other terribly assembled Spanish phrases. People were communicative and enthusiastic about my attempt. I remember driving through the community from the airport to where we were staying out by one of the former fortresses. On the way through the community, I could detect the differences from road to road, from block to block, in terms of who lived there and who was in control of the area.

Fast-forward to a distinct moment where I and my team of about 10 or so colleagues were interviewing restaurant owners, clinic facilitators, and clinic operators. We spent time asking them about what had happened—what their experiences and lessons had been during Hurricane Maria. Our prompt from school was all about the reestablished power within the community, an intentional double entendre, so it included both the electricity—how do we recover and restore electricity?—and how do we account for the political power that does or does not exist within the communities?

We sat down with one shop owner who ran a restaurant and bakery. The bakery was beautiful, adorned in art with a garden out front. It was remarkable, especially compared to the block that it was sitting on where so little else in the way of recovery had been done since the hurricanes. Much of the block was leveled, still just dilapidated, and hadn't been attended to since the hurricanes had occurred. Yet this place was absolutely beautiful.

We asked him to share with us a little bit about why his shop had recovered and the places around him didn't. Of course, he didn't jump right into that. Instead, he shared with us first that when the hurricane hit, the shop was covered in several feet of water. When it was safe to reenter the shop, they were bucketing water out because the walls had served as a levy to hold water inside, instead of, as they were designed to, holding water outside.

He shared that hundreds of people had come together to help, and many stayed for weeks on end. We said, "Okay. That makes sense. The recovery is heroic. But what we don't understand, still, is why your restaurant looks so great, and the restaurant next door doesn't." The restaurant owner got soft-spoken, had a bit of a tear in his eye, leaned down his head, and looked down to the ground. He said, "The first day we cried, but then we got to work."

This attitude was familiar to me. Growing up, my mom used to say, "The obstacles to the job are the job."

The idea here—and I hope the idea conveyed throughout this book—is that we cannot displace humanity for crisis response. We cannot squelch the need for processing time, for denial, for grief, for sadness. We cannot overcome our initial human instincts for the protection of our children, our loved ones, our families first. We cannot overpower our instinct to put somebody else's mask on first without substantial training.

We have to integrate our human reaction and our practical response to an emergency. Then and only then can we begin to take the actions that we've described, to lean into the concepts of default to progress, triage, the concentric circles of safety. To orient ourselves toward leadership and communication. To recognize that, in the absence of data, we all make up stories, and therefore, we need to start dialogue. To color outside the lines and to develop relationships. None of this works unless we are first human and willing to be vulnerable enough to be human before we are emergency responders, before we are involved in an emergency, before we are consumed by an emergency.

My hope is that as you go out and get to work on this, you will first recognize that this is really hard and sometimes scary. You'll feel a sense of analysis paralysis at some point. You'll feel overwhelmed at some point. But you'll first focus on getting your own mask on, you'll focus on getting yourself to physical and then psychological safety, and then you'll work in concentric circles to do the same for people around you over time. You'll recognize that after the emergency happens or as the emergency is unfolding, first you'll cry, if that's what needs to happen, but then you'll get to work. And you'll recognize that, in the planning process, there will be obstacles. Especially in our schools, there will be obstacles ranging from cost, to people, to structures of the education system in America or in the world, depending on where you might be when you read this.

If I can be helpful or if any member of my team can be helpful at any point along the way, I invite you to reach out to us to get some support. And we're more than happy to do so. Otherwise, please read the next couple of sections, and visit the accompanying website for a set of resources that I hope will be helpful and empowering as you get started. In fact, I hope by now you've already gotten started. Perhaps you've already cried, and now, it's time to get to work. **If you remember that the obstacles to the job are the job, you can stay focused, maybe even excited, about tackling them.**

ACTION ITEMS & RESOURCES

Action Items:

- ☐ Hopefully you're reading this book *before*, or worst case *after*, an emergency occurs, not during. Jot down a few ways in which you might inspire your students, staff, faculty, and families, to reestablish community and routine while you're facing the seven days after an emergency has occurred. You don't want to have to brainstorm during the event itself.
- ☐ Go build your network today, before an event occurs so that you have the group on speed dial, and you have relationships established up front. Include any group of principals or leaders who can provide support and understanding.
  - ☐ Find three to five trauma counseling organizations that are near you to have on speed dial. Don't just put them on speed dial on your phone, but call

them, talk with them, consider inviting them to campus to tour and talk about their strategy, and then ensure that you truly can call upon them after a major incident occurs. In the more rural parts of the world, you might have to build a network of individuals. In general, I like to have dozens of counselors available because (1) we might need them all, and (2) they might not all be available when our emergency occurs.

☐ Create an ICS team.
☐ Conduct an annual reunification drill.
☐ Conduct a drill where you test your first-aid team and give them a few different scenarios. Challenge them to determine which category folks might fall into. When we do drills in K–12 schools, we do not use the deceased category because it runs the risk of creating additional trauma in the preparedness process, and the goal is to build confidence, not fear.
☐ Your goal should be to reassess risk at least once per year or any time a major development occurs in the world (e.g. a world war, a global pandemic, a new weapon is introduced) and then to have it audited by an external party roughly once every three to five years. Ideally, you'd have an interdisciplinary party conduct the external audit (your insurance company, a safety consultant, etc.). A free and easy option is to have your police department audit every other year and then your fire department audit on alternating years to get the different perspectives that ultimately create the interdisciplinary kaleidoscope you're trying to look through.

Resources:

☐ IndigoPathway Career Survey: Run a self-assessment to learn about who you are as a leader and as a contributor, and see your stress reactions.

- [ ] One of my favorite principals I've ever interacted with is named Linda Cliatt-Wayman, and she delivered this <u>TED Talk in 2015</u>.[1]
- [ ] <u>The Principal Recovery Network</u>: Established by current and former principals of schools where gun violence has occurred.

For a list of all the resources throughout the book, please visit `https://www.chrisjoffe.com/books/allclear`.

Suggested Reading:

- [ ] *# Never Again*, David Hogg
- [ ] *Catastrophe and Social Change*, Samuel Henry Prince
- [ ] *Choosing Hope*, Kaitlin Roig-Debellis
- [ ] *Dare to Lead*, Brene Brown
- [ ] *Escaping from Slavery*, Francis Bok
- [ ] *Generations*, Meagan Johnson
- [ ] *Lockdown Drills*, Jaclyn Schildkraut
- [ ] *Stop the Killing*, Kate Schweit
- [ ] *Talking with Strangers*, Malcolm Gladwell
- [ ] *The Boy Who Was Raised as A Dog*, Bruce Perry
- [ ] *The Gift of Fear*, Gavin DeBecker
- [ ] *The Unthinkable*, Amanda Ripley

---

[1]"How to Fix a Broken School? Lead Fearlessly, Love Hard," n.d. `https://www.ted.com/talks/linda_cliatt_wayman_how_to_fix_a_broken_school_lead_fearlessly_love_hard?language=en`.

Appendix

J offe Emergency Services serves schools, events, and organizations through staffing of security and medical personnel and consulting through its Learning & Management Practice. Joffe Emergency Services Advisors, who form the vision and cocreate the organizational strategy, include as of today, members of the former FBI Active Shooter Program and safety/executive leaders from UBER, Eye To Eye, KIPP Foundation, KIPP SoCal, US Prisons Bureau, and more.

Joffe Emergency Services has served thousands of schools in their effort to develop safer communities. The uniqueness of Joffe's approach is fundamentally its people strategy. There are many providers who will say something can or can't be done; however, Joffe's people are specifically mission aligned to the clients they serve. They understand the importance, and they work to achieve the greatest possible outcomes in the areas they serve.

For a list of critical events described and referenced throughout the book, please visit `https://www.chrisjoffe.com/books/allclear/incidentperspective`

Index

Page numbers followed by *f* and *t* refer to figures and tables, respectively.